BULLYING

The Bullies, the Victims, the Bystanders

Sandra Harris
Garth F. Petrie

A SCARECROWEDUCATION BOOK

The Scarecrow Press, Inc.
Lanham, Maryland, and Oxford
2003

A SCARECROWEDUCATION BOOK

Published in the United States of America
by Scarecrow Press, Inc.
A Member of the Rowman & Littlefield Publishing Group
4501 Forbes Boulevard, Suite 200, Lanham, Maryland 20706
www.scarecroweducation.com

PO Box 317
Oxford
OX2 9RU, UK

British Library Cataloguing in Publication Information Available

Library of Congress Cataloging-in-Publication Data
Harris, Sandra, 1946–
  Bullying : the bullies, the victims, the bystanders / Sandra Harris, Garth F.
Petrie
    p. cm.
  "A ScarecrowEducation book."
  Includes bibliographical references (p.) and index.
  ISBN 0-8108-4705-1 (Paperback : alk. paper)
  1. Bullying in schools—United States—Prevention. I. Petrie, Garth
F., 1938– II. Title.
LB3013.32 .H37 2003
371.5'8—dc21

2002154515

I AM

I am . . . Curious like a blind man
Given the gift of sight,
Who could never diminish others . . .
Yet others diminish me.
I am . . . one who fears loneliness may
Overcome my life. . . .
Failure may take me
Like a deadly plague.
I am . . . she who needs love
Like an abandoned child,
Sheltered from the dark of the outside world
But I cannot trust, not even my own shadow.
I am . . . he who would never
Betray a friend
Like a cat betrays its master,
But I can cry.

—Lines from student poems posted on the wall
of an alternative high school, March 4, 2002

CONTENTS

INTRODUCTION

"Someday people are going to regret teasing me," said Barry Loukaitis, fourteen, of Moses Lake, Washington. On February 2, 1996, he walked into his algebra class with a hunting rifle, two handguns, and seventy-eight rounds of ammunition. He killed the teacher, two students, and wounded a third.

"I killed because people like me are mistreated every day. . . . I am malicious because I am miserable," said Luke Woodham, sixteen, of Pearl, Mississippi. On October 1, 1997, he killed his mother, then killed two students and wounded seven.

"I just remember life not being much fun," an anonymous shooter said. "'Reject, retard, loser.' I remember 'stick boy' a lot, because I was so thin" (Dedman 2000, 2–3).

On March 6, 2001, just as the horrors of Paducah (Kentucky), Springfield (Oregon), Jonesboro (Arkansas), and Littleton (Colorado) were beginning to recede in America, high school students went to school in Santee, California. At the end of that school day, two boys were dead, and thirteen other students were wounded. Newspaper headlines read, "No motive," but the accompanying story reported that "Williams was occasionally bullied when he lived in Kentucky [and] . . . the teasing and bullying worsened when [he] got to California" (Booth and Snyder 2001, A6).

No one knows at this point exactly what caused Andy Williams, Michael Carneal, Kip Kinkel, Mitchell Johnson, Andrew Golden, or the others to shoot to kill at school, but bullying is frequently mentioned as a possible contributor. In fact, a recent report by the U.S. Secret Service noted that in over two-thirds of school shootings, the attackers had experienced some form of bullying prior to the incident and a number had experienced bullying at school over long periods of time. Equally incriminating was a CNN Gallup poll taken after the Columbine High School shootings in which high school students blamed each other for the constant bullying, teasing, and harassment that sometimes causes young people to react so violently.

We want to emphasize that bullying is not a factor in every case of school violence; certainly, not every child bullied at school will engage in serious violent acts. However, it has only been within the last few years that schools, communities, and parents throughout the world have begun to recognize that bullying is not something that can be dismissed with such comments as "boys will be boys" or admonitions "just to tough it out." Instead, they have begun to look at bullying as a behavior fraught with inherent violence, one that can contribute to a horrific cycle of mayhem at its worst and, at the very least, creates a climate of fear and unhappiness for millions of school children.

Many concerned parents and educators have finally begun to participate in a dialogue that recognizes the potential danger of bullying, and some prevention and intervention programs have been implemented to make our schools safer. As a result, the most recent school crime statistics appear to indicate that related incidents of school violence are lessening. According to a report released in 2001 by the National Center for Education Statistics (NCES) and the Bureau of Justice Statistics (BJS), students in the United States from ages twelve through eighteen were victims of more than 2.5 million total crimes at school in 1999. Approximately 186,000 of these were violent crimes, such as rape, sexual assault, robbery, and aggravated assault; thirty-eight were homicides. This was a reduction from the previous year, when 2.7 million total crimes occurred at school, of which nearly 253,000 were considered violent (Kaufman et al. 2001).

Additionally, between 1993 and 1999, the percentage of students in grades nine through twelve who reported bringing a weapon to school decreased from 12 percent to 7 percent; between 1995 and 1999, students who feared certain locations at school decreased from 9 percent to 5 percent. As a result, the percentage of twelve to eighteen-year-olds who felt unsafe sometimes or most of the time at school has decreased from 9 percent to 5 percent from 1995 to 1999 (Kaufman et al. 2001).

While it is true that these NCES statistics are encouraging, rates have not declined for other school crimes. For example, during the period of 1993 to 1999, the percentage of high school students threatened or injured with a weapon on school property remained at nearly 8 percent. At the same time, students reporting that they had been offered, sold, or given marijuana on school property and illegal drug use increased from 24 percent in 1993 to 32 percent (Kaufman et al. 2001).

Still, this most recent NCES study reported that 10 percent of students in grades six and seven were being bullied, compared with 5 percent of eighth and ninth graders and 2 percent of tenth through twelfth graders. Alarmingly, 13 percent of students ages twelve through eighteen reported being called derogatory words relating to race, religion, disability, gender, or sexual orientation, and 36 percent saw hate-related graffiti at school.

Forty years ago, teachers in public school indicated that the most serious classroom problems were tardiness, talkative students, and gum chewing. Today school faculty identify as some of their most serious classroom problems drugs, gangs, weapons on campus, and the threat of assault, robbery, theft, vandalism, rape, or even murder. Still, one of the most common forms of victimization at school is bullying. In 1995, Shakeshaft and colleagues reported that as many as 4.8 million students in the United States were threatened physically, verbally, and indirectly every year by other students. The National Institute of Child Health and Human Development (NICHD) reported in 2001 that 17 percent of students in grades six through ten had been bullied "sometimes" or "weekly," 19 percent had bullied others, and 6 percent had both bullied and been bullied (Ericson 2001); others have reported that as many as 80 percent of middle school students engaged in some type of bullying behavior yearly. Even more disconcerting is evidence suggesting that as early as kindergarten and first grade, children are at risk of being bullied.

There is no doubt that school violence is a critical problem in America's schools or that bullying is a maladaptive behavior with consequences.

that appear to contribute to this violence. The effects of bullying are far-reaching and include lowered self-esteem, increased absenteeism, depression, inhibited academic performance, and impaired social relationships. Generally, hostile bully behaviors are not exhibited in the presence of teachers or other adults. Often, children who are bullied do not report that they are being victimized. Frequently, even innocent bystanders who see bullying occur do not report what they see. Consequently, bullying is often underreported by young people and unacknowledged or minimized by adults, including teachers and parents, who do not understand the full scope of the problem. Yet, at the national level, there are reports that 10 percent of students who drop out of school do so because they are repeatedly bullied at school (Hamilton 2002).

Clearly, bullying can negatively affect the school experience for the bully, the bullied, and the bystander. In truth, every child who comes under its influence, whether victimized directly or not, is a victim. Bullying can be reduced; by making schools safer, educators create learning communities that nurture the social and academic development of all of their children. But first, educators and parents must recognize the pervasive nature of the problem; only then can the process of prevention begin.

In the following chapters, we report the results of many studies, including some of our own, related to the incidence of bullying at school. While many characteristics of bullies and victims are similar throughout all grades, we have emphasized those that are different or more pronounced at elementary, middle school, and high school levels in respective chapters on those subjects. We explore where and when bullying occurs, characteristics of the bully and the victim, and the consequences for bullies, victims, bullied/bully students, and bystanders. We describe programs and resources that intervene to reduce and prevent bullying. Finally, we focus on how schools, teachers, administrators, parents, and the community can work together to build stronger support systems for America's children. Because recognition of the problem is so necessary, the appendix contains samples of our bully survey for students and of our survey for teachers and administrators. These may be duplicated and revised as needed and are made available to encourage educators to take the first step and gather much-needed data about the level of bullying on their campuses.

REFERENCES

Booth, W., and D. Snyder (2001). No remorse, no motive from shooting suspect. *San Antonio Express-News,* March 7, A1, A6.

Dedman, B. (2000). School shooters: Secret Service findings. *Chicago Sun-Times,* October 15, at www.suntimes.com/shoot/ (accessed March 30, 2002).

Ericson, N. (2001). Addressing the problem of juvenile bullying. *OJJDP Fact Sheet, 27,* June. U.S. Department of Justice, Office of Juvenile Justice and Delinquency Prevention.

IIamilton, A. (2002). Oklahoma passes anti-bullying law. *Dallas Morning News.* May 6, 2002, 1A.

Kaufman, P., et al. (2001). *Indicators of school crime and safety, 2001.* U.S. Departments of Education and Justice. NCES 2002-113/NCJ-190075. Washington, D.C.: Government Printing Office.

Shakeshaft, C., et al. (1995). Peer harassment in schools. *Journal for a Just and Caring Education* 1(1), 30–44.

BULLYING AT SCHOOL: AN OVERVIEW

It is not true that suffering ennobles the character, happiness does that sometimes, but suffering, for the most part, makes men petty and vindictive.

—Somerset Maugham, *The Moon and Sixpence*, 1919

WHAT IS BULLYING?

A strong interest in the behavioral phenomenon of bullying, referred to as "mobbing," began to take form in Sweden in the late 1960s and early 1970s. Daniel Olweus, a Scandinavian researcher generally recognized today as the foremost authority on bullying, began using the terms "bully/victim" and "whipping boy" in his early studies. Today, because of the abusive nature of bullying, it is often referred to as "peer abuse" or "peer harassment." Nonetheless, the most common term, "bully," is widely accepted in research studies throughout the world.

Because bullying is such a complex behavior, it is difficult to define. Frequently it is defined as extreme behavior that is abusive; however, many children experience daily teasing or exclusion that would not meet a standard definition of extreme behavior. Yet these children are so frightened or miserable that they fear going to school. Consequently, Olweus (1991) recommends that an all-encompassing definition of bullying include the following four criteria:

- It is aggressive and intentionally harmful.
- It is carried out repeatedly.
- It occurs in a relationship where there is an imbalance of power.
- It usually occurs with no provocation from the victim.

In this book we define bullying as "intentionally harmful, aggressive behavior of a more powerful person or group of people directed repeatedly toward a less powerful person, usually without provocation."

While young people who bully others are not always aware of how much their behavior bothers the victims, most of them have some realization that intended victims do not like what is happening to them. Australian researcher, Ken Rigby (1996), calls this "malign bullying"— the bully evidently enjoys what he is doing, while the victim feels a sense of oppression or powerlessness. Malign bullying has seven elements:

- There is an initial desire to hurt.
- The desire is acted upon.
- Someone gets hurt.
- A more powerful person or group hurts someone less powerful.
- There is no provocation.
- The behavior is typically repeated.
- The bully enjoys hurting the weaker person.

Nonmalign bullying is more like teasing, a game, "a seemingly harmless practice from which some sort of pleasure is gained" (Rigby 1996, 18). Generally, this bully does not know the harm that is being done; still, it is serious and should not be ignored.

Not all bullying is obvious, as hitting or verbal teasing are. Sometimes bullying is subtle, such as consistently excluding victims from groups and activities. This type of bullying is particularly insidious, because often victims do not realize that they are being bullied. Thus, bullying can be direct and also indirect, as shown here:

Direct Bullying	Indirect Bullying
Taunting, teasing	Influencing others to taunt or tease
Calling names	Influencing others to call others names
Verbally criticizing unfairly	Influencing others to criticize unfairly
Threatening/obscene gestures	Spreading rumors about others
Menacing stares	Making anonymous phone calls
Hitting	Ignoring others intentionally
Using a weapon or threatening to use one	Influencing others to physically hurt someone
Stealing or hiding another's belongings	Excluding others on purpose

The most common form of bullying is verbal—name calling and hurtful teasing. In 1999, about 13 percent of twelve to eighteen-year-olds in the United States reported they had been called derogatory words referring to race/ethnicity, religion, disability, gender, or sexual orientation. Thirty six percent of students saw this type of graffiti at school. This type of bullying behavior occurred equally in urban, suburban, and rural schools. Females reported being targets of derogatory words more than males, and black students were more likely than white or Hispanic students to report being called hate words (Kaufman et al. 2001).

HOW FAR-REACHING IS BULLYING?

Bullying occurs everywhere, but it is particularly prevalent within the school setting. In a Canadian study, adults remembered their most frequent types of childhood abuse as coming not from parents, as child abuse, but from school peers, in abuse (bullying) at school. Many observers make the wrong assumption that bullying is most likely to occur going to and coming home from school. While it does occasionally happen then, bullying is much more likely to happen at school—in the classroom, on the playground, in the hallways, in the restrooms, and in the lunchroom.

Bullying has been studied widely throughout Europe, the United States, Canada, Japan, New Zealand, and Australia. In Japan, Maeda (2000) reported that *Ijime* (very similar to bullying) has become prevalent, indicating that 60 percent of students had experienced bullying either as a bully, victim, or witness. A 1995 Australian study by Rigby and Slee reported that as many as 19.3 percent of boys and 14.6 percent of girls between the ages of ten and seventeen indicated being bullied at least once a week. In 1993, Olweus reported that about 9 percent of Norwegian and Swedish children in grades one to nine were bullied with some regularity at school. Numerous studies in England confirmed that bullying is extensive and have reported that as many as 27 percent of primary school students are bullied "sometimes" or even more frequently. Studies in the United States have reported that as many as 78 percent of children said they had been bullied within the previous month; nearly 10 percent indicated that the bullying was severe (Walls 2000). While these represent only a few of the studies, all conclude that bullying is a serious problem for children.

WHO IS THE BULLY?

While teasing and quarreling between classmates of equal power and popularity is somewhat natural and even appropriate, it is bullying when there is a power difference between the bully and the victim. Students who act as bullies appear to enjoy harassing the same classmates over long periods of time. They appear to gain satisfaction from the pain of their victims and have little empathy or concern for the students being victimized.

While girls more frequently report being bullied than boys, typically boys engage in more bullying behavior and are bullied more often than girls. Additionally, girls are more likely to engage in indirect bullying (excluding someone from being a part of activities), while boys are more apt to use physical bullying, such as hitting or kicking.

Generally, bullying is most likely to occur with ten to fourteen-year-olds and becomes less as children get older. Because bullies are generally identified as older than their victims, there has been concern that older children dominate or bully younger children. While this is often the case, some studies have found that it is not always so. When children are placed in mixed-age groups, they may actually be bullied less, and may even engage in bullying behaviors less, than do children in same-age classes.

Bullies often are of average popularity, and it is not unusual for bullies to operate in groups. While boys who are victims generally identify individuals as the bullies, frequently the bully's behavior is sustained by a supporting group. Bullies are often described as oppositional toward adults, antisocial, and more likely to break school rules than are other students.

While many people excuse the behavior of bullies who appear tough and aggressive as just a manifestation of their insecurity, more often the opposite is true. In most cases bullies demonstrate little anxiety and insecurity and do not suffer from poor self-esteem. Another characteristic of bullies is that they often have parents and guardians who use physical punishment; frequently, their parent/child relationships are poor, resulting in hostility toward their environments.

WHO IS THE VICTIM?

Almost always, the victims of bullies are children on the bottom rung of the social ladder. Typically, victims fall into two categories: passive and provocative. However, most victims of bullying are passive. These children are anxious, insecure, quiet, afraid of confrontation, cry or become upset easily, and have few friends. They suffer from low self-esteem and rarely report the incidents of bullying, because they fear retaliation. Often passive victims are smaller and weaker than the bullies and fearful of standing up to them. Passive victims see themselves as unattractive, stupid, and as failures. They have little sense of humor and sometimes are described as depressed, although they usually cause little trouble when at school due to this passivity.

Provocative victims are more active, assertive, and somewhat more confident. While still anxious, these victims are more reactive emotionally. They tend to tease and annoy classmates until they retaliate. However, when provocative victims fight back, they are usually ineffective but will prolong the fight even if they are losing. These victims may have a learning disability or so lack social skills as to be insensitive to other students. Daniel Olweus describes the provocative victim as generally the least popular person with classmates, because their classroom behavior is often so disruptive that everyone reacts negatively to them.

WHAT ARE THE CONSEQUENCES FOR THE BULLY?

Often bullies perceive their "misplaced" power status as increased prestige and have a sense of being in control. However, this uneven power relationship between the bully and the victim can have damaging effects for the bully. For example, adults who admit to having bullied others at school have reported experiencing greater degrees of depression than do adults who did not bully others at school.

Children who have been identified as school bullies have a much higher chance of later dropping out of school, committing delinquent acts, being convicted for drunken driving. Additionally, they treat their own children and spouses with more aggression and greater severity than those who have never indicated that they were bullies. In fact, their children are more likely to become bullies, thus continuing this cycle of abuse. Olweus reported in a 1991 study that 60 percent of students identified as bullies in grades six to nine had criminal convictions by the age of twenty-four. In fact, Garbarino (1999) suggests in his book *Lost Boys: Why Our Sons Turn Violent and How We Can Save Them* that boys become bullies to "compensate for their experiences of victimization at home" (p. 193).

WHAT ARE THE CONSEQUENCES FOR THE VICTIM?

Experiences of being bullied appear to have long-term effects on children, including lowered self-esteem, increased absenteeism, depression, and suicide. School attendance is affected; many studies report that bullied children stay away from school out of fear. Even more so, the constant emotional distress of bullying can effect academic performance. Bullied students often have a diminished capacity to learn due to the stress of fear and consequently perform more poorly on academic tests. Additionally, bullied students are less satisfied with school, in general, than are their peers.

Bullying also interferes with the social and personal development of children, which can lead to social isolation and encourage dropping out of school. Often a bullied child does not have a single good friend in his or her class, contributing to a sense of isolation. The reaction of sadness rather than anger can become worse for the victim, because these students have fewer adaptive responses for dealing with bullying, even blaming themselves. Rigby reported that even students who were bullied frequently but said it did not bother them tended to see themselves as unpopular and had fewer friends than other students in the school.

Rigby (1996) suggested that there is indirect evidence of a link between suicide and peer victimization at school. He cited the tragic story of an Australian youth who hanged himself and left a suicide note that attributed his desire to, among other factors, having been repeatedly bullied at his school. Another example from our own experience happened in Georgia when a student shot himself in front of his classmates.

Research on abuse within families consistently demonstrates that the abused are likely to become abusers when they have families of their own, leading to the suggestion that children who are bullied are more likely to become bullies themselves. In fact, a study of Finnish children ages eight through twelve indicated that children who are victims of bullying are often involved in bullying four years later. Similarly, a recent study found that while students with low self-esteem are more likely to be bullied, these students can then begin to bully others. This type of bully falls into another category, the "bully/victim." Bully/victims are victims of bullying who admit to bullying behavior. These children appear to be at risk of remaining involved in bullying longer than any other group of children. Fried and Fried (1996) tell of an example in an interview with an identified bully in prison who claimed that he had started bullying his peers because he felt so powerless when a boy his age beat him up. Finally, in the seventh grade, he "refused to be a victim any longer . . . and started bullying the bullies" (p. 92).

WHAT ARE THE CONSEQUENCES FOR THE BYSTANDER?

A large group of children generally ignored when considering the problem of bullying comprises children who witness bullying—the bystanders. According to Richard Hazler (1996), bystanders see what is happening yet do not understand what is occurring well enough to deal with their own emotional reactions. Nor are they able to construct strategies to prevent the bullying behavior. Typically, educators who address the bullying problem try to help the victim and punish the bully yet ignore the bystanders.

Observing another child being bullied frequently causes conflicting emotions in the bystander—anger, sadness, fear, and indifference. Bystanders feel guilt when they cannot help the victim and fear that the same thing might happen to them. Interestingly, research has found that victims and bystanders react similarly physiologically. In fact, both victims and bystanders in contact with violence over a period of time begin to repress feelings of empathy for others, a response that desensitizes them to negative behaviors at school. Thus, even bystanders who do not know what they should do are fearful of becoming the brunt of a bully attack and fear that they might do the wrong thing, which could cause more problems.

HOW DO ADULTS PERCEIVE BULLYING?

Parents in general feel that bullying is completely inappropriate and that it should be stopped. If it is their child being bullied, parents tend to want punitive action, while school counselors tend to believe that bullies can be encouraged to change their behavior. Curiously, some parents appear actually to admire a bully, especially if their sons or daughters. Generally, though, parents are more unaware of a bullying problem at school and rarely talk about it with their children.

There is a perception among some students that telling adults will not help, because their intervention is too little, not effective, and may even cause the bullying to become worse. Generally, bullied children, as well as bystanders, do not report incidents of bullying, because they fear retaliation or are not sure if teachers and administrators in their schools are even interested in trying to stop bullying. Too often, teachers feel that bullying issues should be dealt with by the administration or by counselors. Other teachers express a desire to help reduce bullying incidents on their campuses but admit they do not really know how to do it.

CAN INTERVENTIONS REDUCE THE PROBLEM OF BULLYING?

Daniel Olweus was among the first to examine the nature and incidence of bullying. In the 1970s, he explored this phenomenon in Sweden and

Norway and persuaded authorities to begin a national campaign to reduce bullying. Two years later, studies indicated that bullying had been reduced in some schools by as much as 50 percent and that the longer the program was in effect the school climate continued to improve. However, bullying cannot be dealt with by isolating the problem of bullies and their victims on a school campus; instead, effective interventions must focus on the school climate as a whole. Olweus (1991) identifies the following six factors as being necessary in any approach to reducing bullying at school:

- Identify the extent of the problem on a campus through a campus wide questionnaire.
- Begin a parental awareness campaign.
- Involve students and teachers in developing class rules and implementing them.
- Develop individualized interventions with bullies and victims.
- Implement cooperative learning activities.
- Increase adult supervision.

A successful prevention program must intervene on three levels, beginning with the whole school, moving to the classroom, and building relationships with students to address individual needs. Early identification plays a critical role in helping children who have been exposed to violence. In fact, early intervention by a supportive adult may negate the need for professional help later. Programs in which adults are available for all of the victims of bullying—the bully, the bullied, and the bystander—play a critical role in reducing the negative effects of bullying.

REFERENCES

Fried, S., and P. Fried. (1996). *Bullies and victims*. New York: M. Evans.

Garbarino, J. (1999). *Lost boys: Why our sons turn violent and how we can save them*. New York: Free Press.

Hazler, R. (1996). *Breaking the cycle of violence: Interventions for bullies and victims*. Bristol, Pa.: Accelerated Development, Inc.

Kaufman, P., et al. (2001). *Indicators of School Crime and Safety, 2001*. U.S. Departments of Education and Justice. NCES 2002-113/NCJ-190075. Washington, D.C.: Government Printing Office.

Maeda, R. (2000). *"Ijime": An exploratory study of a collective form of bullying among Japanese students.* Paper presented at the Biennial Meeting of the Society for Research in Child Development. Albuquerque, N. Mex., April 1–18, 1999.

Olweus, D. (1991). Bully/victim problems among schoolchildren: Basic facts and effects of a school-based intervention program. In D. Pepler and K. Rubin (eds.), *The development and treatment of childhood aggression.* Hillsdale, N.J.: Lawrence Erlbaum.

Olweus, D. (1993). *Bullying at school.* Cambridge, Mass.: Blackwell.

Rigby, K. (1996). *Bullying in schools: And what to do about it.* London: Jessica Kingsley.

Rigby, K., and P. Slee. (1995). *Manual for the peer relations questionnaire (PRQ).* Adelaide: University of South Australia.

Walls, L. (2000). Bullying and sexual harassment in schools. *Committee for children: Leaders in prevention education,* at www.cfchildren.org.

2

BULLYING IN THE ELEMENTARY SCHOOL: THE PROBLEM

"The teacher put us in a circle and told us we had to hold hands to play this game. My family had just moved to the city and it was my first day of second grade. I didn't know anyone. When I put my hand out to the boy next to me, he said loudly, 'Yuk, your hand's dirty, I'm not holding hands with you!' Everyone laughed. My teacher did not say a word, she just came over and took my hand. Later, on the play- ground, even the girl I sat with on the bus that morning wouldn't play with me. It wasn't until my family moved out of state a couple of years later that kids quit making fun of me or asking if I had washed my hands lately. I only remember two things from elemen- tary school . . . being bullied and feeling sad."

—*Gail, thirty years old*

Generally, it is at the elementary school level that aggressive behaviors of children are first exhibited and addressed by teachers and adminis- trators; increasingly, however, elementary principals are reporting that aggressive behavior is becoming evident in students in preschool through the fifth grade. In preschool and day-care settings, children are most often bullied by being hit, having mean things said to them, and in general being picked on repeatedly by other children. While at these very young ages it appears that bully behavior patterns are directed at more submissive children, even very young children are becoming more aggressive. For example, in 1998 two Florida kindergarten students were arrested for destroying school property and attacking school personnel. Relatedly, two eight-year-olds in Indiana were arrested for carrying handguns to school (Hooks 1999). While these incidents are examples of extreme behavior, many cases of student-to-student physical violence, painful teasing, vandalism, and other bully behaviors are documented daily in elementary schools throughout the world. The following includes a few examples of studies that have reported on bullying in the elementary grades worldwide:

- In Scandinavian countries, 11.6 percent of boys and girls reported being bullied in grades two to five (Olweus 1993).
- Twenty-seven percent reported being bullied "sometimes" or even more frequently in England and Wales (Whitney and Smith 1993).
- In Italy, 42.6 percent reported being bullied "sometimes" or even more frequently (Fonzi et al. 1999).
- Eighteen to 27 percent reported being bullied in Australia (Rigby 1996).
- Thirty-five percent of students in grades four to six reported that they had been bullied at school in the last year in the United States (Berthold and Hoover 2000).

In the United States generally, bullying decreases as children get older: however, there is no doubt that bullying is a problem for elementary-aged children regardless of where they attend school. In fact, several studies (Berthold and Hoover 2000, Olweus 1993, Zumkley 1994) have found that there is a relationship between aggressive children as young as eight and aggression in adults up to thirty years old. The early onset of bullying and victimization behaviors gives additional credence to psychologist Dorothea Ross's suggestion that children entering kindergarten (or perhaps even sooner) could be at high risk for being bullied and should be trained to cope before they ever enter school.

Even seemingly simple bullying behavior can lead to violence, especially when children are subjected to these behaviors frequently. While children react in many different ways to violence, based on their level of development, some common responses among children in preschool through second grade (Pynoos and Nader 1988) are:

- Feeling helpless
- Generalized fear
- Confusion
- Difficulty identifying what is bothering them
- Inability to verbalize their experience
- Regressive symptoms, such as thumb sucking
- Clinging and reluctance to be away from a parent or other adult figure

Children in third through fifth grade tend to respond to violence in the following ways (Pynoos and Nader 1988):

- Impaired concentration and learning
- Feeling responsible and guilt related to the event
- Fear of being overwhelmed by feelings of sadness or anger
- Sleep disturbance
- Concerns about their own and others' safety
- Altered or inconsistent behavior, often aggressive or reckless

ELEMENTARY SCHOOL BULLYING

Gathering data about bullying incidents is often difficult with young children, for many reasons. For example, adults and children often do not define bullying the same way; this can limit the reliability of the questionnaire approach even when a survey is read to children. Therefore, it is important to explore children's understanding of the topic and use their vocabulary when phrasing questions.

Often, young children use the word *teasing* more often than *bullying*, especially when describing verbal acts of aggression that hurt. A study by Khosropour and Walsh (2001) noted that when children were asked to describe what a bully was like they consistently said that bullies were like people who tease. They defined bullies as "people who do the teasing. A lot of times they pick on a single person and tease and tease so that person then tries to tease back. That ends up turning the person who's been teased into a teaser" (p. 19).

There is a general belief that children are singled out for peer abuse because of how they look—such as being overweight, dressing poorly, or wearing glasses—but this is not typically so for younger elementary-aged children. Instead, victims tend to be passive, insecure, and submissive around their peers, or anxious, aggressive, immature, and impulsive—such as children with special needs. However, as children reach the fourth and fifth grades, their bullying targets are often specifically those with particular physical traits (such as size) and behavioral characteristics (such as being easily angered). For example, girls are more likely to indicate that kids who are bullied are of different ethnicities or do not dress nicely, while boys are more likely to make fun of other children who wear glasses.

Elementary children, especially those being bullied frequently, are more likely than older children to tell adults about being bullied, but still the majority of bullying incidents go unreported. When elementary victims do report that they are being bullied, they occasionally report that the bully is a girl, but most often the bullies are boys; rarely are they mixed groups of boys and girls. Most children at this age are bullied by being called bad names, teased, lied about, hit, isolated, threatened, having their things stolen, or being left out of activities. Typically, the most common locations for elementary students to be bullied are the school's playground and the classroom.

Based on research by Borg (1999), Olweus (1993), Rigby (1996), Whitney and Smith (1993), Berthold and Hoover (2000), and others, this is some of what we know about elementary-aged victims:

- The number of victims seriously bullied decreases as students get older.
- The number of female victims declines more rapidly than that of male victims.
- More young victims report being beaten up, threatened, isolated, and lied about than older victims.
- Victims may be average, above, or below average with regard to school achievement.
- Victims tend to be anxious and lack assertiveness.

- Victims consider themselves less able than parents believe they are, compared to students who have not been bullied.
- Victims report feeling sad more often than students who have not been bullied.
- Victims feel more afraid at school than their peers.
- Victims feel that they are unable to defend themselves effectively.
- Younger victims are more likely to report that they are being bullied than older victims are.

Elementary bullies are more likely to report that they have bullied at this age than they will as they get older. Young male bullies tend to be more overtly aggressive, such as hitting or openly teasing, while female bullies engage in more relational aggression, such as trying to damage another child's friendships or withdrawing from a play group.

This is some of what we know about bullies in the elementary school:

- There are no particular trends in the number of young bullies who actually engage in frequent or serious bullying.
- Younger bullies are most likely to victimize others on the playground, on the way to school, and on the way home than older bullies.
- Younger bullies are significantly less likely to bully in the classroom than older bullies.
- Younger bullies are less likely to resort to name calling or threatening than older bullies.
- Younger bullies are more likely to lie about, hit or kick, or exclude others than older bullies.
- Elementary-school bullies are likely to be more popular than bullies in the higher grades.
- Younger bullies admit to more antisocial behaviors, such as drinking, smoking, and cheating, than their peers.
- Younger bullies attend school less frequently than older bullies and less frequently than other children generally.

Even children in elementary school can be so badly affected by bullying that they consider suicide. Rigby (1996) tells of an eight-year-old girl who attempted suicide at home "after she had complained of being repeatedly harassed at school by a group of other girls" (p. 57).

Another disturbing by-product of bullying is the effect it has on the attitudes of bystanders, children who see bullying happen but are not directly affected by it. These children often admit that they can imagine themselves bullying another student, especially one they do not like. At the same time, most young bystanders report a general reluctance to help other students being victimized.

LONG-TERM EFFECTS OF BULLYING

There is general agreement that victims of bullying of all ages experience physical ailments, emotional problems, lowered self-esteem, and scholastic difficulties. Additionally, students who are victims of bullying in the elementary grades often report being bullied several years later; this appears to be more true for boys than for girls.

While elementary bullies are likely to have friends, by the time they enter high school they have become less popular than other students and are more likely to drop out of school than their peers. Nan Stein (1995) has found that children who engage in bully behavior in elementary school are also more likely to take part in sexual harassment and assaults in high school, as well as in adulthood. Moreover, as mentioned earlier, aggressive patterns of behavior developed in childhood tend to continue into adolescence and adulthood. For example, former bullies are more likely to have trouble with law enforcement officials and to require mental health services than other adults. One study followed a group of highly aggressive third graders for twenty-two years; by the age of thirty, 25 percent already had criminal records, while only 5 percent of their peers did (Eron et al. 1987).

WHAT OUR ELEMENTARY BULLYING STUDY FOUND

We surveyed 433 fifth graders at four elementary schools in rural Texas and Georgia. The students surveyed included 180 boys and 253 girls. Children participating in this study were Hispanic (53), African American (109), Anglo (236), and other (35).

How Often Does Bullying Happen at Your School? Nearly 63 percent of the students surveyed indicated that bullying occurred at their schools at least "sometimes," while 27 percent reported that bullying happened "often" or "all the time." Yet when asked how often they themselves had been bullied, over half indicated that they were never bullied, while 15 percent reported that they were bullied "weekly"; another 15 percent said they were bullied "daily." At the same time, at least 20 percent of these elementary students said that they did "not feel very safe" at school. Encouragingly, though, nearly 80 percent reported at least "usually" feeling safe at school.

Where or When Does Bullying Happen at Your School? The four most common (at least "sometimes") places/times that elementary students observed bullying at school were at recess (78 percent), in the hallway (52 percent), in the restroom (50 percent), and in the classroom (43 percent). These were followed by on the way home from school (40 percent), on the way to school (34 percent), and on field trips (18 percent).

What Kinds of Bullying Do Elementary School Students Experience? Students reported the following kinds of bullying as happening "at least sometimes":

- Being called names (76 percent)
- Having rumors spread about them (74 percent)
- Being teased (70 percent)
- Being left out of activities (66 percent)
- Being hit or kicked (62 percent)
- Having things stolen (42 percent)
- Being threatened (41 percent)

In these four schools, the differences relating to gender were minimal in every category.

How Do Elementary School Students Feel after They Have Been Bullied? Twenty-two percent of students reported that they had been bullied but that it had not bothered them, while 5 percent indicated it made them feel "mostly frustrated." Yet 20 percent reported it made them feel "angry" (more boys than girls) and another 9 percent (more girls than boys) commented it made them feel "sad."

We then asked students if they had ever had thoughts of getting back at the bully, and 78 percent responded at least "sometimes." In fact, 30 percent of boys and girls indicated that they had these types of thoughts "all the time." Generally, the most likely way that students would "get back at bullies" was by no longer being their friends.

CONCLUSION

Clearly, bullying at the elementary school level is a problem that must be addressed. Yet educators generally have been more concerned with addressing bullying at the upper grades than at the elementary level.

REFERENCES

Berthold, K., and J. Hoover (2000). Correlates of bullying and victimization among intermediate students in the Midwestern USA. *School Psychology International* 21(1), 65–78.

Borg, M. (1999). The extent and nature of bullying among primary and secondary schoolchildren. *Educational Research* 41(2), 137–53.

Eron, L., et al. (1987). Aggression and its correlates over 22 years. In D. H. Crowell, I. M. Evans, and C. R. O'Donnell (eds.), *Childhood aggression and violence*, pp. 249–62. New York: Plenum.

Fonzi, A., et al. (1999). Italy. In P. K. Smith, Y. Morita, J. Junger-Tas, D. Olweus, R. Catalano, and P. Slee (eds.), *The nature of school bullying: A cross-national perspective*, pp. 140–56. London: Routledge.

Hooks, M. (1999). *Existence of and responses to violence in Georgia elementary schools.* Unpublished dissertation. Georgia Southern University.

Khosropour, S., and J. Walsh (2001). *That's not teasing—that's bullying: A study of 5th graders' conceptualization of bullying and teasing.* Paper presented at the Annual Conference of the American Educational Research Association, April 6, 2001: Seattle, Wash.

Olweus, D. (1993). *Bullying at school.* Cambridge, Mass.: Blackwell.

Pynoos, R. S., and K. Nader (1988). Psychological first aid and treatment approach to children exposed to community violence: Research implications. *Journal of Traumatic Stress* 1(4), 445–73.

Rigby, K. (1996). *Bullying in schools: And what to do about it.* London: Jessica Kingsley.

Ross, D. (1996). *Childhood bullying and teasing: What school personnel, other professionals, and parents can do.* Alexandria, Va.: American Counseling Association.

Stein, N. (1995). Sexual harassment in school: The public performance of gendered violence. *Harvard Educational Review* 65, 145–62.

Whitney, I., and P. Smith (1993). A survey of the nature and extent of bullying in junior/middle and secondary schools. *Educational Research* 35(1), 3–25.

Zumkley, H. (1994). The stability of aggressive behavior: A meta-analysis. *German Journal of Psychology* 18(4), 273–81.

3

ELEMENTARY SCHOOL BULLYING PREVENTIONS AND INTERVENTIONS

"The four elementary school children who first came to me with their wonderful ideas [about reducing bullying at school] were fourth grade students at the West Haverstraw Elementary School[,] . . . now commonly called 'The Friendship Village.'"

—*Roberto Calderin, assistant principal at School 9 in Yonkers, N.Y.*

The best way to solve bullying problems is to teach children how to *prevent* bullying in the first place. Because bullying is a learned behavior, it is critical that these aggressive behaviors be addressed at their earliest stages, when they can be unlearned. Since most researchers believe that children internalize ideas about what is acceptable and unacceptable by the time they are eight, it is generally recommended that behavior-intervention strategies be used as early as two years old, when most youngsters begin acquiring skills for resolving frustration.

However, when bullying problems already exist, there are a variety of interventions to consider that specifically address the needs of young children. Whether the action involves prevention or intervention to reduce bullying, we believe that there must be three understandings:

- Bullying of any kind is a serious problem for all involved.
- Adults (parents, counselors, teachers, administrators, community members) and children must be involved together in addressing bullying.

- An integrated approach that influences the entire school climate is necessary to bring about long-term results.

The most effective efforts to prevent bullying focus on measures that help children feel cared for, secure, and able to form attachments. Thus, a critical factor in promoting children's social development is bonding with positive, nurturing adults (Gregg 1998). Another important factor for elementary children is to promote social development so that they understand the importance of friendships and, quite simply, how to be a good friend. In order to do this, some educators advocate a separate curriculum that promotes social competencies for K–6 children, while others recommend integrating prosocial behaviors into the overall school environment. With this in mind, we believe that the most effective intervention/prevention strategies involve the entire learning community. They include:

- Creating a climate at school that is affirming and safe
- Communicating appropriate behavior standards to children
- Helping children learn positive interpersonal skills.

CREATING A CLIMATE AT SCHOOL THAT IS AFFIRMING AND SAFE

While all school faculty members must accept the challenge to keep our schools safe from bullying, the elementary principal is most frequently identified as the individual who must lead the challenge to ensure safety at school. In fact, schools characterized as safe invariably are led by principals who foster an atmosphere based on the principles of belonging and caring among students, faculty, and parents. Educators who recognize the negative effect of bullying on the entire school climate are vigilant and convey the need for vigilance to the entire school campus.

Elementary principals, counselors, and teachers committed to preventing bullying at school establish an affirming, safe climate by:

- Being visible throughout the building
- Being accessible to students, staff, and parents

- Committing themselves to supporting and understanding student needs
- Involving children and parents in creating policies that govern student behavior
- Communicating standards of behavior to all of the school community
- Consistently helping students adhere to rules and school policies
- Supervising areas of the school building and grounds at all times
- Holding the school community responsible for maintaining a safe, respectful, learning environment

Just as bullying is a learned behavior, respect is also a learned behavior. Likewise, adults have a great influence in shaping children's understandings of norms and values related to both of these concepts. When adults are openly against all forms of bullying and are committed to consistently modeling behavior respectful of others, children internalize these same behaviors. For example, Cypress-Fairbanks School District, a large suburban district in northwest Houston, Texas, demonstrates its commitment to reducing bully behaviors at school by training teachers and other staff to work with the bully, the victim, and the bystander. Additionally, Superintendent Rick Berry invites students and parents to sign a STAR (Students Tell an Adult Right Away) pledge at the beginning of each school year (see Appendix A).

COMMUNICATING APPROPRIATE BEHAVIOR STANDARDS TO THE CHILD

Discipline That Emphasizes the Positive

Schools must adopt a policy that clearly communicates that bullying is not allowed. No behaviors are to be dismissed with the attitude of "kids will be kids." Instead, bullying is recognized as an inappropriate behavior that often leads to violence. Bullying must be clearly defined, and this definition must be posted schoolwide. At the elementary level we would recommend the following definition: "Bullying is: teasing that is unpleasant, being called hurtful names, being hit or kicked, being left out on purpose, and having rumors spread about you."

Discipline policies, often called codes of conduct, are necessary for schools that intend to communicate clearly the expected appropriate behaviors and the consequences that follow when these behaviors are not used. Yet too often, consequences for bullying focus on punishment alone; adults fail to counsel a child in learning appropriate behaviors. Generally consequences only deal with the offender, which means that the bully gets in trouble and has a consequence assigned, but nothing is done to help the victim or other bystanders. Thus, discipline policies must make a balanced effort that includes components to counsel the bully, the victim, and bystanders in order to address underlying reasons for bullying behavior. In other words, emphasis on discipline must stress right behavior for all instead of just focusing on reprimands and punishment for wrong behavior.

Discipline procedures are most effective when teachers deal with the bully and with the victim separately, quietly, and in private, helping the bully understand the full implications of the behavior and encouraging him or her in more appropriate ways to interact with others. The teacher must work with the victim, counseling in appropriate responses to different forms of bullying. Also, bystanders who failed to act appropriately must be provided responsible ways of responding, including telling an adult.

The behavior contract, an agreement between the school principal or the teacher and the misbehaving student, is a common strategy for elementary students. Generally, the contract is written in positive terms in which the bully agrees to refrain from bullying behavior over a predetermined time frame. The contract also specifies a reward for the student who produces a positive outcome. Providing students with rewards for prosocial behavior often will deter aggressive behavior. Behavioral contracting can be used with victims also. For example, the bullied child could agree to ignore teasing or use other, carefully explained, appropriate responses.

Discipline with Sanctions

Even at the elementary level, stricter disciplinary policies for violent behavior, which includes bullying, are being adopted. While many of these policies support serious sanctions, rarely is out-of-school suspension used at this level. In the most severe cases of bullying, it may be necessary to remove children from school or provide them with alternative placements. Lakeland, Florida, has established an alternative placement school for young children where the needs of aggressive students in kindergarten through second grade are addressed. The purpose of this program is specifically to work with disruptive primary-aged students to develop positive interpersonal skills that will help them be successful in the regular classroom setting (Barbosa and Gilpin 1998). Few districts can offer such an alternative facility; they might consider a special class at school, led by the counselor, for children involved in serious bullying.

In-school suspension, staffed with certified personnel who focus on student accountability and responsibility, is a sanction often used in cases of serious incidents of bullying at the elementary level. This disciplinary strategy is most effective when it is accompanied with counseling and encouragement of students to develop better means of communication and interpersonal skills. "Timeout"—removing a child from school activities—is a common strategy for disciplining young students who engage in forms of bullying behavior. Most experts recommend that children assigned to timeout not serve longer than two minutes per the age of the child (Hooks 1999).

CHARACTER AND CONFLICT MEDIATION PROGRAMS

Moral growth appears to occur when connections with other individuals are strengthened. In fact, when working with children to learn positive interpersonal skills, it is important that the value of community be emphasized in ways that promote responsibility to and for others (McHenry 2000). To encourage this sense of community, many schools have adopted character education programs that focus on morals and ethics for personal growth. An important component of character education programs is that of stressing the importance of friendships and the process involved in building relationships that result in friendships.

Another intervention/prevention strategy involves conflict-resolution and peer-mediation programs, which have been adopted by many districts in an effort to help children resolve problems without resorting to bullying behaviors. The purpose of these programs is to empower students and provide them with skills to mediate differences among their classmates. This is done by training a group of responsible, mature students in strategies that help them to moderate conflicts among children having difficulty getting along. For elementary children, conflict-resolution and peer-mediation programs are rarely used in isolation; instead, teachers incorporate components of these programs into the curriculum and into the social structure of the classroom. Peer-counseling programs tend to gain support from other students, who are generally more responsive to suggestions from other students than they are to adult interventions.

RESOURCES TO REDUCE BULLYING

Examples and descriptions of bully resources that are specifically designed for elementary school-aged children are listed below. These programs, videos, books, and websites represent only some of the excellent resources that are available.

School Curricula

Broome, S., and N. Henley (2000). *Teaching character . . . It's elementary: 36 weeks of daily lessons for grades K–5.* Character Development Publishing. This is a format for integrating a student goal, a relevant quote, and a related character trait across the curriculum.

Garrity, C., et al. (1995). *Bully proofing your school: A comprehensive approach for elementary schools.* Longmont, Colo., telephone (800) 547-6747. This is a comprehensive anti-bullying program based somewhat on the work of Daniel Olweus. It provides overhead transparencies and other resources.

Daniel the dinosaur. Published by the Johnson Institute in Minneapolis, telephone (800) 231-5165. This program is designed to help K–6 victims of bullying.

Derman-Sparks, L. (1989). *Anti-bias curriculum: Tools for empowering young children.* Washington, D.C.: National Association for the Education of Young Children. This book is developed for those who work with children two years and older; it provides resource material.

First step to success. Published by Center for Effective Collaboration and Practice, and at cecp.air.org/resources/success/firststep.htm and www.sopriswest/com, telephone (303) 547-6757. Designed for kindergarten students. This program has three major components that include kindergarten-wide screening for at risk behavior, the classroom-based CLASS curriculum, and HomeBase, which involves families in the intervention process.

Freiberg, H. J. *Consistency management and cooperative discipline (CMCD)*. University of Houston, College of Education, Houston, Texas 77204-5872, telephone (713) 743-8663. This is a schoolwide program designed to improve discipline in inner-city schools for grades K–6. This program emphasizes shared responsibility between students and teachers and brings them together to make rules for classroom management.

Koenig, T., and B. Meyer (1999). *Caring kids: Social skills & character education lessons for grades 1–3*. Thinking Publications. This is an elementary curriculum that stresses cooperative learning and role playing to help children express their feelings appropriately.

No-bullying. Developed for grades K–8 by the Johnson Institute, telephone (800) 231-5165. This program emphasizes the importance of adult intervention in bullying.

PATHS (Promoting Alternative Thinking Strategies). Developmental Research and Programs, telephone (800) 736-2630, and www.drp.org/paths.html. Designed for use with kindergarten through fifth grade. This program develops emotional and social competencies and helps reduce aggression.

Quit it: A teacher's guide on teasing and bullying. Wellesley College's Center for Research on Women, telephone (781) 283-2510. This curriculum is designed to help children in grades K–3 rethink behaviors that contribute to a bully culture.

Peace Builders. Heartsprings, Inc., telephone (800) 368-9356, and www. peacebuilders.com. Designed for use in kindergarten through fifth grade. It promotes five principles: praise others, avoid put-downs, seek wise people as friends, notice and correct hurts that one causes, and right wrongs.

Resolving Conflicts Creatively Program. RCCP National Center, New York, N.Y., telephone (212) 509-0022, e-mail esrccp@aol.com. This program trains educators to provide students with instruction in peer mediation and reducing bias. It also works with parents to resolve conflicts nonviolently at home. Students in fourth to sixth grades serve as mediators in disputes.

Robertson, J. (ed.). (1999). *Teaching for a tolerant world*. National Council of Teachers of English, telephone (800) 369-6283. Developed for teachers of grades K–6, this collection of twenty-four essays focuses on tolerance.

Second step. Published by Client Support Services at Committee for Children, telephone (800) 634-4449. Designed for students in prekindergarten through eighth grade. This program incorporates social skills techniques into the regular school day and encourages students to control their own behavior and to understand other people. *Second Step* has a six-week parental involvement component to train parents of elementary-school students in strategies to be reinforced at home.

Sjostrom, L., and N. Stein. *Bullyproof: A teacher's guide on teasing and bullying for use with 4th and 5th grade students.* Wellesley College's Center for Research on Women, telephone (781) 283-2510. Teacher's guide with eleven sequential lessons to give students the opportunity to explore and determine the distinctions between "teasing" and "bullying."

Just for Children

Gainer, C. (1998). *I'm like you, you're like me: A child's book about understanding and celebrating each other.* Free Spirit. Developed for grades pre-K to three, this text focuses on diversity and encourages young children to learn concepts of acceptance, kindness, cooperation, and respect.

Keller, H. (2000). *That's mine, Horace.* Greenwillow. Picture book for grades pre-K to two, about respect and honesty.

Langreuter, J., and V. Sobat (1998). *Little bear and the big fight.* Millbrook. Picture book developed for pre-K through second grade, this book is about friendship and forgiveness.

Lewis, B. (2000). *Being your best: Character building for kids 7–10.* Free Spirit. This book focuses on ten character traits that include cooperation, caring, relationships, and citizenship. A leader's guide is also available.

Marshall, J. (1999). *George and Martha.* Perfection Learning. This book for grades K–1 is a collection of five short stories that explores how to create and maintain friendships.

Polland, B. (2000). *We can work it out: Conflict resolution for children.* Tricycle Press. This book developed for children in grades K–3 explores constructive solutions for everyday problems related to getting along with others.

Spelman, C. (2000). *When I feel angry.* Albert Whitman. Developed for grades pre-K through second, this picture book helps young children understand how to deal with anger. It also discusses appropriate reactions to bullying.

Professional Books

Beane, A. (1999). *The bully-free classroom.* Free Spirit. Teacher resource book for grades K–8.

Boatwright, B., T. Mathis, and S. Smith-Rex (1998). *Getting equipped to stop bullying: A kid's survival kit for understanding and coping with violence in the schools.* Educational Media, e-mail emedia@usinternet.com. Designed for all levels. Its aim is to provide an understanding of the dynamics of bullying and to empower children to recognize and deal with bullies at a young age, in order to minimize later problems.

Dobrin, A. (1999). *Love your neighbor: Stories of values and virtues.* Scholastic. Designed for parents of elementary children, it includes thirteen original animal fables that focus on themes, such as, friendship, loyalty, prejudice, and responsibility.

Zarzour, K. (2000). *Facing the schoolyard bully: How to raise an assertive child in an aggressive world.* Firefly Books. Developed for parents and educators of children of all ages, the focus of this book is understanding what causes children to become bullies and developing appropriate interventions.

Videos

Bully no more: Stopping the abuse. (1999). AIMS Multimedia. Designed for use with grades four to six. This videocassette reveals how to keep from being a target of bullies, how to stop bullies, how to get help for them, provides advice for bystanders. The teacher's guide includes reproducible student activities.

Courtesy Counts. (1999). MarshMedia, telephone (800) 821-3303. Designed for grades K–3; an action video showing elementary students behaving in courteous ways and in not so courteous ways.

Got a problem? Solve it! Sunburst, telephone (800) 431-1934. Videocasette with teacher's guide. Developed for grades two to four.

Sticks and stones: Let's talk about teasing. (1995). Human Relations Media, telephone (800) 431-2050. Videocassette for grades two to five, features kids responding to teasing and offers appropriate alternatives for dealing with this situation.

Student workshop: Don't be so bossy. (2002). Sunburst Technology, at www.sunburst.com. This video introduces children in grades K–2 to basic assertiveness skills and teaches them how to stand up for themselves. It encourages children to accept differences, be empathetic, and be assertive.

Websites

Anti-Bullying Handbook, at www.vuw.ac.nz/education/anti-bullying/. This site includes information on bullying and bullies for children.

Building Character, Inc., at www.buildincharacter.org. A character education resource and training center with links to related associations.

Bullying, at www.bullying.co.uk. Offers advice about bullying for teachers, children, and parents.

Bully-Busters, at www.insideouted.com.aul. Offers leaders, parents, and children self-esteem techniques and strategies to deal with bullying.

Center for the Fourth and Fifth Rs, at www.cortland.edu/www/c4n5rs. Disseminates articles relating to the teaching of character traits, such as respect, responsibility, and caring.

Center for the Prevention of School Violence, at www.ncsu.edu/cpsv/. Nationally recognized information resource about prevention of school violence.

Hurt Free Schools, at www.hurt-free-character.com. Uses character education and social skills training to create safe environment for bully prevention in the elementary school.

Kidscape, at www.Kidscape.org.uk/. Offers help, information and publications for parents and schools on keeping kids safe from abuse.

The North Carolina Character Education Partnership, at www.dpi.state.nc.us/nccep. Features a searchable database of children's literature, model lesson plans integrating character education across the curriculum, and a procedural guide documenting community consensus, curriculum integration, and school climate.

REFERENCES

Barbosa, S., and A. Gilpin (1998). Six-year old placed under house arrest. *Macon Telegraph*, February 22, 9.

Gregg, S. (1998). *School-based programs to promote safety and civility.* AEL Policy Briefs. Charleston, W.Va.: Appalachia Educational Laboratory.

Hooks, M. (1999). *Existence of and responses to violence in Georgia elementary schools.* Unpublished dissertation. Georgia Southern University.

McHenry, I. (2000). Conflict in schools: Fertile ground for moral growth. *Phi Delta Kappan* 82(3), 223–27.

Schmidt, T. (1996). *Daniel the dinosaur learns to stand tall against bullies: A group activities manual to teach K–6 children how to handle other children's aggressive behavior.* Minneapolis, Minn.: Johnson Institute.

4

BULLYING IN THE MIDDLE SCHOOL: THE PROBLEM

"The thing I remember most about Middle School was being bullied—
not by everyone, but this one guy really must have hated me! At the
beginning of the year when I was in 7th or 8th grade, I wore these
tennis shoes that my Mom bought for me. And this guy made so much
fun of my shoes—every time he saw me, he would laugh really loud,
point at my shoes, and say in this high sing-song voice: 'Jake's got
brand new tennies, cheap, cheap!' It got so bad that if I saw him com-
ing, I would go another way, even if I was late to class. I finally told
my Mom and when she got paid that week, she went out and bought
me these really expensive new tennis shoes. But he still made fun
of me. . . . I guess it wasn't just my shoes."

Jake C., now twenty-four years old

The middle school years are a difficult time for youngsters, no matter
who they are. One 7th grader tells about being bullied all year long because of the way she looked, and especially about her glasses. She was
excluded from parties, ate lunch by herself every day; no one spoke to
her at school. Now, years later, she characterizes her peers at that time
as "the meanest people I ever met."

Certainly, for many youngsters, the middle school years are characterized as a time of difficulty and confusion, and much of this is attributed

to poor peer relationships. In fact, it is almost impossible to have a conversation with a middle schooler or with anyone about their middle school years in which the subject of bullying is not mentioned in some fashion. This unpleasant phenomenon of bullying does not just occur in U.S. middle schools; in fact, it occurs worldwide:

- In Norway, Olweus (1993) estimated that 15 percent of students in junior high schools were involved in bully/victim problems with some regularity.
- In England, 10 percent of secondary students reported being bullied at least sometimes.
- In Japan, 13 percent of lower secondary students were victims of *Ijime,* bullying (Morita et al. 1999).
- In the United States as many as 10 percent of middle school students reported being bullied during the past six months (Kaufman et al. 2001).

Throughout most of the United States, middle school represents a new school configuration. Students are no longer part of the familiar neighborhood elementary school; instead, several elementary schools feed into one, usually larger, middle school. At the same time, the school day is considerably different. Instead of having one teacher most of the day, sixth graders are often scheduled with six or seven different teachers and see their homeroom teacher rarely. This new school structure often contributes to bullying behavior as middle school students try to establish dominance in the new grouping.

Even without considering the issue of bullying, the middle school years, when young people are approximately eleven to fourteen and in grades six to eight, are generally described as a time of great risk socially, as well as emotionally. At this time, students often need help learning to identify, acknowledge, and manage their emotions and their actions; many, quite naturally, feel a sense of isolation. Therefore, it is especially important for parents and teachers to establish a climate at home and at school that fosters a sense of belonging and encourages adolescents to form strong associations with adults, as well as peers.

However, bullying engenders destructive behaviors that form barriers to positive connections with other individuals, young or old. For example, some middle school boys and girls consider that bullying others causes them to be admired. Other students justify this behavior by saying that some kids just "deserve to be bullied"; while some actually admit that bullying makes them "feel good." Researchers Hoover and Oliver (1995) reported that students agree that the most trauma from bullying occurs during the middle school years and suggested that as many as 80 percent of middle school students engage in bullying behaviors. Clearly, bullying has negative consequences for all children—the bully, the victim, and the bystander, but it is particularly painful for adolescent children in their middle school years.

MIDDLE SCHOOL BULLYING

Based on research studies by Nansel et al. (2001), Salmon (1998), Hoover and Oliver (1995), Ma (2001), Kass (1999), Miller et al. (2000), Limber et al. (1998), Olweus (1993, 1996), Rigby (1996), and others, this is some of what we know about the victims of bullying in the middle school:

- Victims have poorer psychosocial adjustment than those who are uninvolved.
- Victims demonstrate poorer social and emotional adjustment than bullies.
- Victims report greater difficulty making friends than bullies.
- Victims have poorer relationships with classmates than do bullies.
- Victims feel greater loneliness than bullies.
- Victims are more anxious than bullies.
- Victims are more likely to have low academic status than bullies.
- Victims are likely to use alcohol, smoke, and be poor academic achievers.
- Victims are usually physically different in race or size, or wear different clothing than bullies.
- Victims are often reported as not being as good at things as others.
- Victims indicate the degree of school satisfaction or dissatisfaction is related to how much they are bullied physically or psychologically.

- Victims usually have lower self-esteem than bullies.
- Special-needs children are particularly at risk.

While bullied students often exhibit some of the same characteristics as their victims, there are clear differences; some characteristics are more often found in bullies than in their victims. This is some of what we know about middle school bullies:

- Bullies have poorer psychosocial adjustment than those who are uninvolved.
- Bullies are more likely to use alcohol and smoke than their victims.
- Bullies are more poorly adjusted to school both academically and in their perceptions of the school climate than their victims.
- Bullies make friends more easily than their victims.
- Bullies are rarely as socially isolated as their victims.
- Bullies are generally always more popular than their victims.
- Bullies often tease other students to go along with the crowd but admit this sometimes makes them feel uncomfortable.
- Bullies say the main reason for bullying students is that "[the victims] just don't fit in."
- Bullies in later middle school years appear to have poorer self-esteem than their victims.

It has long been suggested that children who are bullied become bullies, and there is evidence that in some cases this is so. Therefore, another category of bullying to consider is that of students who admit they have been bullied by others who also admit to being bullies— often referred to as "bully/victims." In fact, Ross (1996) has found that approximately 6 percent of seriously bullied children admit to bullying others. Some of the characteristics of these middle school bully/ victims include:

- Bully/victim students exhibit the poorest adjustment socially and emotionally of all.
- Bully/victim students exhibit the greatest problem behaviors.

- Bully/victim students often have poor physical conditions, yet they target physically weaker students.
- Bully/victim students, especially boys, feel a need to retaliate.

Richard Hazler (1996) has identified a fourth group of children in middle school who further exacerbate the issue of bullying, the bystanders. Often, bystanders do not help victims but feel guilty because they think they should. Other bystanders do not help the victim because even in middle school they feel it is "none of their business." Some of what we know about how bullying affects bystanders is:

- Bystanders rarely get involved, for fear of being next.
- Bystanders rarely get involved, for fear of doing the wrong thing.
- Bystanders report a feeling of powerlessness.
- Bystanders appear to suffer a loss of self-respect.
- Bystanders lose their confidence over time.
- Bystanders become desensitized to bully behaviors
- Bystanders in middle school become less sympathetic toward bully victims, especially boys.

LONG-TERM EFFECTS OF BULLYING AND BEING BULLIED

There is no doubt that the negative effects of bullying and being bullied reach into adulthood. For example, we know that:

- Bullies, as well as bully victims, are likely to drop out of school.
- Over time, the popularity of bullies tends to decrease, and by high school they are significantly less popular than other students.
- Bullies are four times as likely as other students to be involved in criminal behavior by the age of twenty-four.
- Students who were victims of bullying in early grades report also being bullied several years later.
- Victims of bullying in middle school often are more depressed and have poorer self-esteem by the age of twenty-three, even though they are no longer harassed or socially isolated.

- Chronically victimized students may even be at increased risk for other mental health problems, such as schizophrenia and suicide.

WHAT OUR BULLYING STUDY FOUND

We surveyed 131 boys and 67 girls in the eighth grade at two middle schools in Texas. Both schools were fairly large, enrolling over 1,000 students each. The ethnic breakdown of students who participated in our study was 26 percent African American, 35 percent Hispanic, 35 percent Anglo, and 4 percent other. (For a complete report of our middle school study, see Harris and Petrie 2002.)

How Often Does Bullying Happen at Your School?

This question explored how often students saw bullying at their school and how often bullying had actually happened to them within the last year. Fifty-nine percent of students indicated that "sometimes" bullying occurred, and an additional 33 percent reported it happened "often." Thus, an amazing 92 percent indicated that bullying happened at least "sometimes."

It is much easier for students to admit that they "see" bullying than it is for them to admit that they themselves have been or are being bullied. In fact, while 92 percent of middle schoolers in our study admitted that they saw bullying happen at their school, only 36 percent reported that they had been bullied sometime within the past year. Still, most students indicated that they felt safe at school, with only 11 percent of students (more girls than boys) saying that they did not "feel very safe."

Where or When Does Bullying Happen?

The majority of students reported seeing bullying at least "sometimes":

- At lunch (83 percent)
- In the classroom (77 percent)
- At extracurricular events (63 percent) (Significantly more boys than girls)

- On the way home from school (62 percent)
- At recess (61 percent)
- On the way to school (34 percent) (Significantly more boys than girls)

What Kinds of Bullying Do Students Experience?

Middle school students reported "at least" sometimes:

- Being called names (49.5 percent)
- Being teased unpleasantly (46.5 percent)
- Being left out of things (34 percent) (Significantly more girls than boys, and more Hispanic students than African-American or Anglo students)
- Being hit or kicked (22 percent)
- Being threatened (20 percent)

Both Olweus (1996) and Rigby (1996) reported that twice as many boys as girls report being threatened or hit or kicked; however, we found that more girls (22.4 percent) than boys (19 percent) actually reported being threatened and that nearly as many girls reported being hit or kicked.

How Do Students Feel after They Have Been Bullied?

Of middle schoolers who admitted to being bullied, 11 percent reported that bullying made them feel "miserable," and 23.5 percent said it made them feel "angry." As expected, boys were much more likely to report feeling "angry," while girls were most likely to say they felt "miserable." Bullying at school also contributed to school absences. In fact, while only 4 percent said that they had actually stayed home from school at least once or twice because they were afraid of being bullied, 17 percent said that they had thought about doing so.

Whom Do Students Tell about Bullying?

Over half of bullied students do not tell anyone about their bullying experiences at school. When they do tell, they are most likely to tell a friend or their mother; only 3 percent of students said that they would tell their father or a teacher. When students did tell someone else about being bullied at school, only 23 percent felt that it got better; 18 percent said that things stayed the same; and 6.5 percent felt that the bullying became even worse.

When we asked middle school students to tell us how interested they thought their teachers and administrators were in reducing bullying on their campuses, it became clear why they did not tell school faculty. An overwhelming majority viewed teachers (59.5 percent) and administrators (73 percent) as "not interested" or "didn't know" if they were interested or not. At the same time, nearly 80 percent of girls and 57 percent of boys believed they should work together with their teachers and administrators on this problem.

CONCLUSION

Data from our study of two Texas middle schools are very consistent with other studies that indicate that bullying at the middle school level is a problem. Our findings also support other studies that have indicated that bullying actually increases at the middle school level (Harris, Petrie, and Willoughby 2002, Harris and Petrie 2002, Hoover and Oliver 1995).

REFERENCES

Harris, S., and G. Petrie (2002). A study of bullying in the middle school. *NASSP Bulletin* 86(633), 42–53.

Harris, S., G. Petrie, and W. Willoughby (2002). Bullying among 9th graders: An exploratory study. *NASSP Bulletin* 86(630), 3–14.

Hazler, R. (1996). *Breaking the cycle of violence: Interventions for bullying and victimization.* USA: Accelerated Development, Taylor & Francis Group.

Hoover, J., and R. Oliver (1995). *The bullying prevention handbook: A guide for principals, teachers, and counselors.* Bloomington, Ind.: National Educational Service.

Kass, S. (1999). Bullying widespread in middle school, say three studies. *APA Monitor* 30(9), 1–2, at www.apa.org/monitor/oct99/cf3.html.

Kaufman, P., et al. (2001). *Indicators of school crime and safety: 2001*. U.S. Departments of Education and Justice. NCES 2002-113/NCJ-190075. Washington, D.C.: Government Printing Office.

Limber, S., et al. (1998). Bullying among school children in the United States. In M. Watts (ed.), *Cross-cultural perspectives on youth and violence: Contemporary studies in sociology* 18, pp. 159–73. Stamford, Conn.: Jai Press.

Ma, X. (2001). Bullying and being bullied: To what extent are bullies also victims? *American Educational Research Journal* 38(2), 351–70.

Miller, D., et al. (2000). Bullying in a school environment and its relationship with student satisfaction, performance, and coping reactions. *Psychology: A Journal of Human Behavior* 37(1), 15–19.

Morita, Y., et al. (1999). Japan. In P. Smith, et al. (eds.), *The nature of school bullying: A cross-national perspective*. London: Routledge.

Nansel, T., et al. (2002). Bullying behaviors among U.S. youth: Prevalence and association with psychosocial adjustment. *Journal of American Medical Association* 285(16), 2094–2100.

Olweus, D. (1993). *Bullying at school: What we know and what we can do*. Oxford: Blackwell.

——— . (1996). Bully/victim problems in school: Facts and effective intervention. *Reclaiming Children and Youth* 5(1), 15–22.

Rigby, K. (1996). *Bullying in schools: And what to do about it*. London: Jessica Kingsley.

Ross, D. (1996). *Childhood bullying and teasing: What school personnel, other professionals, and parents can do*. Alexandria, Va.: American Counseling Association.

Salmon, G. (1998). Bullying in schools: Self reported anxiety, depression, and self-esteem in secondary school children. *British Medical Journal* 317, 924–25.

5

MIDDLE SCHOOL BULLYING PREVENTIONS AND INTERVENTIONS

On May 27, 2000, Christian (not his real name) started off to school with his friend. In his friend's backpack was a rifle. A neighbor saw the rifle and contacted the police. Now Christian stood in a living room, sobbing and holding a gun to his head as police officers tried to talk him into putting it down. For a few moments he thought that he might take his own life; instead he handed the rifle to the police. Then Christian and another twelve-year-old were arrested in a plot to kill two fellow students who had been bullying them at their middle school (Clack 2002, E-1).

By the time children reach middle school, bullying has become its most intense. However, children of this age are far less likely than elementary children to report to any adult that they are being bullied, unless strong bonds have already been formed. In fact, unless middle schools are organized with a critical emphasis on the building of relationships, a serious mismatch will exist between the school organization and the needs of its young adolescents.

There is no doubt that a safe environment is necessary to promote learning at school. Students must have a school with a secure, supportive environment, free from violence and disharmony, one that promotes tolerance and respect for all of its students, and that enjoys the involvement and support of the entire community. Educators, working hand in hand

with parents and other community members, must cooperate in this responsibility to establish school learning communities that emphasize
socially acceptable behavior. In doing this they must agree on three important understandings:

- Bullying is not acceptable behavior.
- All adults must work together to address bullying within their
  community.
- Collaboration, in the framework of an integrated, long-term approach,
  can influence children's behavior and reduce incidences of bullying.

If these three principles are not followed, bullying incidents such as the
one reported at the beginning of this chapter will occur all too often.
Christian had told his mother about being bullied daily, and she had
tried to transfer him to another school in the district. But this had not
worked, and so Christian and his friend had resorted to what appeared
to them at the time the only way to end the bullying—more violence.

Just as with younger children, the most effective efforts to prevent
bullying focus on strategies that build with other children and adults relationships that contribute to a healthy learning environment. Healthy
relationships are key ingredients for adolescents in the process of being able
to learn. But for young adolescents, this need for attachment becomes even
greater; it expands to a need for belonging to a peer group (Jackson and
Davis 2000). Consequently, middle schools have been encouraged to create
learning communities that foster healthy relationships and at the same time
address bullying. Some of the organizational changes involved are:

- Serving smaller numbers of students, approximately six hundred
- Restructuring larger middle schools into schools-within-schools or
  "houses"
- Teaming teachers and students
- Flexible scheduling, allowing students to spend blocks of time with
  particular teachers
- "Looping," which allows students and teachers to keep teams in
  place for several years
- Creating advisory periods for students and teachers, which often
  develops interpersonal bonds

For middle school students the most effective intervention/prevention strategies involve the entire learning community in a way that:

- Creates a climate that is affirming and safe at school
- Communicates appropriate behavior standards to the students
- Helps students learn positive interpersonal skills

CREATING A CLIMATE THAT IS AFFIRMING AND SAFE

Because of the uniqueness of middle school students, it is important for success to provide them with principals and teachers who have received specialized preparation, not just in teaching but in teaching and working with children specifically in the middle grades. These educators should be skilled in:

- Understanding the emotional and social developmental needs of adolescents
- Understanding the academic skills needed
- Implementing instructional strategies that best suit this age group
- Participating actively in the lives of middle school students
- Involving parents and community members in the learning community

Middle school educators who have been comprehensively trained to work with adolescents are well on their way to being able to address not only academic needs but those that arise out of bullying-related conflicts.

Project-based learning, or cooperative learning, is a recommended strategy for relationship building in the middle school. This approach to instruction provides opportunities for children of different socioeconomic backgrounds, different ethnicities, and cultures to interact within the safe setting of the school. Slavin (1995) reports that many deep, long-lasting crosscultural friendships have begun in cooperative learning groups.

Issues dealing with racial and ethnic differences are increasingly critical during the middle school years (Jackson and Davis 2001). Adolescents who are bullied because of prejudice find their opportunity for belonging, so important at this age, severely undermined. Therefore, it is important that curriculum in the middle grades reflect a wide variety of ethnic groups; further, substantive conversations about issues of race and ethnicity should be encouraged, with trained adult guidance.

The amount and quality of supervision is another necessary component in creating a school that is bully-free. Talking with students or conducting a simple survey at school can locate problem areas. Generally, these areas are hallways, playgrounds, restrooms, and, surprisingly, the classroom itself. It is not enough for a teacher just to be "on duty" in a high-risk area; a teacher who is actively supervising can often prevent bullying from occurring. While extra supervision is generally not very popular with teachers, who are already overburdened, it is an effective short-term measure in reducing bullying.

COMMUNICATE APPROPRIATE BEHAVIOR STANDARDS TO THE MIDDLE SCHOOL CHILD

Develop Common Expectations for All Students' Behavior

Schools that are genuinely committed to reducing bullying understand that it is not enough to discipline the bully for inappropriate behavior without working with victims and bystanders. All of those involved must be encouraged to develop positive strategies for appropriate behaviors, and this is most likely to happen when schools develop codes of conduct that offer discipline management plans for a whole-school discipline policy.

The all-school code of conduct should clearly identify good and bad behavior and indicate consequences for both. Also, the code should give clear direction regarding what to do when inappropriate behavior is observed. Bullying should be addressed within the code of conduct framework. Few schools now have anti-bully policies in place; instead, most schools refer to bullying behaviors under the term "harassment" or address it in very limited ways, such as, "verbally or physically taunting or bullying other students." The entire school community, including principal, teachers, students, and parents should have an opportunity to contribute to the code of conduct. Once the code has been developed and accepted, it should be communicated to all of the school community. Faculty should go over the code with students and explain that it is everyone's responsibility to enforce it.

A clear definition for bullying at this level should be included in the code of conduct, something like the one given in chapter 1 of this book: "Bullying is intentionally harmful, aggressive behavior of a more powerful person directed repeatedly toward a less powerful person, usually without provocation." This should be followed by a list of bullying behaviors, including harmful teasing, name calling, hitting, threatening, using a weapon, stealing, spreading rumors, ignoring others intentionally, and excluding others on purpose.

The creation of student support teams is one way to support the reduction of students' bullying behaviors. One goal of the support team is to identify ways to work with bullies, victims, and bystanders. Support teams are made up of administrators, teachers, guidance counselors, the school nurse, and other community based health service agencies. This group meets periodically to discuss the needs of the students referred by teachers; when necessary, it writes a plan of action that involves one or more of the team members and takes up the matter with the student, parents, and teacher.

Make Positive Discipline Suggestions

Hoover and Oliver (1995) suggest "behavioral contracting" as one disciplinary approach that contributes to appropriate behavior. The behavior of bullies must be spelled out in a positively worded contract and must include a promise to refrain from specific behaviors that constitute bullying. Contracts can also be created for victims, outlining strategies to ignore bullying and providing more appropriate responses to bullying behavior.

Another recommended activity is that of reverse role playing. This is a helpful exercise to further the understanding of bully, victim, and bystander in a bullying episode. Reverse role playing can also help children develop feelings of empathy (Hoover and Oliver 1995).

Self-monitoring is also a valuable positive strategy, in which the student tallies his or her own aggressive actions, such as name calling, hitting, etc.

A variation of this is to have the bully list times when he or she acted appropriately.

Use Discipline with Sanctions

Sanctions or consequences must be applied consistently and fairly to students who break the rules and bully others. In addition to pointing out to the offender that the behavior is not allowed, assigning consequences also sends a message to the entire school that affirms the school's commitment to providing a safe environment for all students. Consequences range from mild (such as extra duties around the school, or loss of privileges, such as field trips) to severe (which could include detention, in-school suspension, out-of-school suspension, alternative placement, and ultimately expulsion).

Today, zero-tolerance policies require immediate expulsion for violent acts of bullying, such as bringing a weapon to school or attacking other students. Out-of-school suspension for serious bullying behavior cannot keep a student out of school for longer than ten days, and it is rarely used with middle school students. In-school suspension is a more common consequence for serious bullying behaviors at this age, since the student can be kept under the supervision of professionals.

Alternative schools often serve as an alternative setting for students whose behavior is seriously disruptive and are considered "a last resort" to being expelled. Generally, these schools attempt to return students as soon as possible to regular schools.

The ultimate goal of any discipline policy should be a safe and caring school, and assigning consequences or sanctions alone will not do that. Therefore, we recommend that even when consequences are the natural outgrowth of stated discipline infractions, positive counseling should be included to encourage misbehaving students to understand their own behavior and respond more appropriately in the future.

HELPING MIDDLE SCHOOL CHILDREN
LEARN POSITIVE INTERPERSONAL SKILLS

Conflict between students is a natural part of the school day, but it does not have to be disruptive. The purposes of peer mediation and conflict resolution programs are to help students use conflict in a constructive way to solve interpersonal problems and promote a supportive climate for learning. Typically, peer mediation and conflict resolution are especially effective in teaching middle school students anger management and improved communication skills. In fact, conflict resolution is often referred to as "the Fourth R"—reading, 'riting, 'rithmetic, and resolution!

Conflict-resolution programs usually are of two types: programs where disputes are settled by the individuals involved; and programs where a mediator works with those involved to reach a mutually acceptable solution. Conflict resolution has the following key ingredients:

- Active listening
- Summarizing what each party has said to ensure accurate comprehension
- Creative, mutual problem solving

Peer mediation adds an important component to resolution, that of a neutral, impartial student. Schools may be set up in ways such that students may seek mediation by themselves; alternatively, the mediation process may be a part of a disciplinary strategy, which students are referred by peers, teachers, or administrators. Mediation typically involves the following steps:

- The mediator explains the process.
- All must agree that the rules will be followed.
- The mediator asks each disgruntled party to explains his or her point of view.
- The mediator asks follow-up questions.
- The mediator leads a brainstorming conversation with the disputants.
- The mediator asks disputants to decide which solutions would be the most effective.
- The mediator asks each party to restate what has been agreed upon and writes up the agreement. The disputants sign the agreement, pledging that they will abide by it (Jackson and Davis 2001).

An important part of peer mediation is that mediators be trained to have a broad understanding of possible strategies. Another important aspect is that mediators should represent different groups within the school, even mediators who have themselves had behavioral problems or been involved in conflicts.

Another strategy that many schools consider is to implement character education within the curriculum. This can be done in a variety of ways, such as creating an "empathetic school" (Hoover and Oliver 1995), where the focus is on the idea of being "my brother's keeper." These schools teach the worth of fellow classmates throughout the school day. Other schools focus on a specific character trait, such as honesty, for a week or longer, then go on to the next quality.

"Bibliotherapy," reading about other students who have faced being bullied and how they handled the situation, is another way to infuse the curriculum with teaching opportunities. In this process middle school children read books about preventing bullying through coping strategies, imagination, finding protectors, and humor. A recommended book for bibliotherapy is *The boy who lost his face,* by David Sacher (1989), which tells about a boy who is influenced by others to harass an elderly woman. After doing so, he feels guilty and realizes the importance of standing up for his own beliefs rather than following the crowd. (For an excellent discussion and guide for bibliotherapy, see chapter 9 in Hoover and Oliver [1996], *The bullying prevention handbook,* Bloomington, Ind.: National Educational Service.)

RESOURCES TO REDUCE BULLYING

Bully resources that are specifically designed for middle school students are listed below. These programs, videos, books, and websites represent only some of the excellent resources that are available.

School Curricula

Aggressors, victims, and bystanders: Thinking and acting to prevent violence. Education Development Center, (800) 225-4276. Curriculum is composed of twelve classroom sessions dealing with violence among peers and roles of aggressors, victims, and bystanders. Includes the Think-First Model of Conflict Resolution. Designed for middle school students.

Anger coping program. Contact John Lochman, Dept. of Psychology, Box 870348, University of Alabama, e-mail jlochman@gp.as.ua.edu. This is a model for male middle school students who demonstrate aggressive behavior. Lessons emphasize self-management, self-monitoring, perspective taking, and social problem-solving skills.

Basis. Contact Denise Gottfredson, Dept. of Criminology, Room 2220, University of Maryland, e-mail dgottfredson@bss2.uimd.edu. This model focuses on discipline procedures for middle schools.

Bullying prevention project. Contact Susan Limber, Project Director, Bullying Prevention Project, University of South Carolina, (803) 737-3186. This model helps school staff and parents identify and intervene with bullies and their victims.

Developing good character: Guidelines for making responsible decisions. (1999). Meeks Heit Publishing, (800) 821-3303. This multimedia program focuses on ten character attributes, through four complete lesson plans. It includes a video kit with a videocassette, lesson plans, study guides, student worksheets, tests, and transparencies. Designed for grades six through ten.

Doing the right thing: A series about character education (1997). United Learning, (800) 424-0362. This series features scenarios that focus on character issues, such as positive leadership skills, and self acceptance. It includes four videocassettes, four teacher's guides, and four sets of transparencies. Designed for grades seven through ten.

Erlbach, A. (1999). *Worth the risk: True stories about risk takers plus how you can be one, too.* Free Spirit, (800) 735-7323. This program is divided into three parts that identify the meaning of risk taking and understanding the difference between positive and negative behaviors. It includes twenty stories of young people taking risks, such as sticking up for someone.

Family Matter (2000). Perfection Learning, ISBN 0-7891-5084-0. This resource addresses specific questions and thinking skills that focus on how we are influenced by family and how families deal with problems. Each section includes readings, short stories, poems, articles, and writing activities. Designed for grades six through nine.

Kidder, R. (1997). *Building decision skills.* Institute for Global Ethics, (800) 729-2615. Curriculum kit that includes curriculum notebook, audio tape, and video tape. Kit is organized into ten basic lessons that focus on ethics and morals. Designed for grades seven through twelve.

Positive Adolescent Choices Training (PACT). Contact Betty Yung, Director, Center for Child and Adolescent Violence Prevention, Wright State University, e-mail byung@desire.wright.edu. This program is designed for middle and high schools and is a recommended model for high-risk African American youth and other high-risk youth with conduct problems or histories of victimization. Uses video vignettes and role playing to learn positive social skills.

Responding in peaceful and positive ways (RIPP). Contact Aleta Meyer, Life Skills Center, Virginia Commonwealth University, Richmond, Va., (888) 572-1572. This program is for grade six. Its key elements include problem solving, identifying feelings, handling differences, dealing with prejudice, and avoiding, ignoring, defusing, and resolving conflicts.

Sadlow, S. (1998). *Advisor/Advisee character education: Lessons for teachers and counselors.* Character Development, (919) 967-2139. This is a collection of twenty-four character-education lessons to be used by teachers and counselors at the middle school level. The lessons focus on such traits as respect, kindness, and fairness. Conflict resolution is also a topic.

Just for Middle School Students

Espeland, P., and E. Verdick (1998). *Making every day count: Daily readings for young people on solving problems, setting goals, and feeling good about yourself.* Free Spirit, ISBN 1 57542-047-3. This handbook for teenagers provides daily readings featuring inspirational quotes, comments on the quotes, and suggested appropriate actions for every day of the year.

Just for Parents

Zarzour, K. (2000). *Facing the schoolyard bully: How to raise an assertive child in an aggressive world.* Firefly, ISBN 1-55209-456-1. This book addresses questions such as, what causes children to become bullies, why are some children targeted by bullies, and what should parents do if their child is a bully.

Professional Books

Early warning, timely response: A guide to safe schools. www.ed.gov/offices/OSERS/OSEP/earlywrn.html. Research-based practices designed to assist schools in identifying warning signs early in order to develop prevention and intervention response plans.

Karres, E., and E. Shearin (2000). *Violence proof your kids now: How to recognize the 8 warning signs and what to do about them.* Conari Press, ISBN 1-57324-514-3. This handbook identifies eight warning signs of youth violence—alienation, negative friendships, destructive downtime, and others—along with strategies to address the problem.

Marsh, V. (1999). *True tales of heroes and heroines.* Alleyside, ISBN 0-917846-93-1. This is a collection of twenty original stories that use storytelling, paper cutting, mystery-fold, sign language, story puzzles, and other creative strategies to tell the stories of such heroes as Louis Braille, Walt Disney, Christopher Reeve, Sequoya, and Harriet Tubman. Each story includes activities and resources.

Peaceful schools. (1998). Northwest Laboratory. Contact NWREL, Planning and Program Development, 101 S.W. Main Street, Suite 500, Portland, OR 97204 (503) 275-0666. Offers an overview of current research on school violence prevention and outlines practical ideas for classroom use.

Romain, T. (1998). *Cliques, phonies, and other baloney.* Free Spirit, ISBN 1-57542-045-7. This is a guide for helping young people make and keep friends. The author uses humor, direct advice, and cartoons; for grades two through seven.

Videos

Manners matter. (1999). MarshMedia, (800) 821-3303. This video uses comical live-action role reversal in the home and at school to reinforce how important it is to consider others, take turns, be a good sport, otherwise use good manners.

Student workshop: All about respect. (1997). Sunburst, (800) 431-1934. This is a video kit with one videocassette, twenty-seven reproducible handouts, and a teacher's guide. It features scenarios that deal with respecting others' feelings, respecting differences, and other related topics. Discussion questions are included. Designed for grades six through eight.

Conflict resolution for youth: Programming for schools, youth-serving organizations and community and juvenile justice settings—satellite teleconference. (1996). (800) 638-8736. This is a videotaped teleconference that promotes the incorporation of conflict resolution strategies into programming for schools and other settings.

Websites

(Most websites have information or links for a wide variety of grade levels.)

Center for the Advancement of Ethics and Character, www.web.bu.edu/sed/caec/home-desc.html. This site supports character education through research and publications addressing teachers and teacher training, as well as providing resources for educators and parents.

Character Education Partnership (CEP), www.character.org. CEP is a national resource center that disseminates information of programs designed to develop moral character and civic virtue.

Character Counts! www.character-counts.org. Nationwide nonprofit initiative that supports character education through teaching trustworthiness, respect, responsibility, fairness, caring and citizenship. Comprehensive website includes a section in Spanish.

Office of Juvenile Justice and Delinquency Prevention (OJJDP), www.ojjdp. ncjrs.org/. Provides national leadership, coordination, and resources to develop, implement, and support effective methods to prevent juvenile victimization and respond appropriately to juvenile delinquency.

U.S. Department of Justice for Kids and Youth, www.usdoj.gov/kidspage/. Information for youth on crime prevention, staying safe, and community service opportunities, among other things.

References

Clack, C. (2001). A boy is ready for life to go on after it came so close to ending. *San Antonio Express-News,* May 25, E-1.

Jackson, A., and G. Davis (2001). *Turning Points: 2000.* New York: Teachers College Press.

Hoover, J., and D. Oliver (1995). *The bullying prevention handbook.* Bloomington, Ind.: National Education Service.

Sacher, D. (1989). *The boy who lost his face.* New York: Trumpet Club.

Slavin, R. (1995). Enhancing intergroup relations in schools: Cooperative learning and other strategies. In W. D. Hawley and A. W. Jackson (eds.), *Toward a common destiny: Improving race and ethnic relations in America.* San Francisco: Jossey-Bass.

6

BULLYING IN THE HIGH SCHOOL: THE PROBLEM

March 6, 2001: Fifteen-year-old Charles "Andy" Williams brought a .22-caliber revolver to school and fired thirty bullets during a rampage in which two schoolmates died and thirteen others were wounded. Friends think that because he had been bullied in Maryland, he and his father had moved to California. "But the teasing and bullying worsened. . . . [P]eople accused him of being gay, . . . they made fun of him for being a country boy, for his big ears. It didn't matter what he did, they made fun of him" (Booth and Snyder 2001).

June 21, 2002: Charles "Andy" Williams pleaded guilty to two counts of first-degree murder and thirteen counts of attempted murder. Defense attorneys said he had endured frequent bullying ("Teen pleads guilty" 2002).

August 15, 2002: Charles "Andy" Williams was sentenced to fifty years in prison for killing two students and wounding thirteen others at his high school. "If I could go back to that day, I would never have gotten out of bed," he said through his tears ("Fifty years to life for school shooting" 2002).

Overall juvenile crime rates are moderating; notwithstanding, according to a recent Public Agenda Report, American teenagers have "alarmingly high rates of violence" (*Violent Kids* 2000, 3) compared with youths of other major nations. For example, an American teenager is ten times more likely to commit murder than a teenager in Canada. Girls are also becoming more violent, with their rate of committing violent acts increasing nearly 36 percent faster than that of teenage boys. Blame for this disturbing trend is complex, and many possibilities are mentioned, including the popular culture, media coverage, mental health issues, availability of guns, etc. But one recurring theme continues to be the anger generated by bullying within our schools. With this in mind, U.S. Secretary of Education Rod Page, in a March 11, 2001, interview with CBS's *Face the Nation*, expressed his concern about the "amount of alienation and rage in our young people."

Despite the level of some acts of violence, we are mindful that not all students who are bullied resort to extremes. In fact, as students get older and enter high school, there is generally a decline in the amount of bullying, as well as a clear trend toward less physical bullying. Still, bullies, victims, and bully/victim students all demonstrate poorer psychosocial adjustment than do youths not involved in bullying (Nansel et al. 2001).

According to Stanford University professor Linda Darling-Hammond, the difficulties that high school students encounter are frequently related to the mismatch between adolescent developmental needs and the kinds of experiences provided at school. At a time when students need to build relationships, they find themselves in large, often depersonalized schools; they are rarely provided opportunities to learn how to make wise choices; and learning often stresses how many facts students can memorize rather than being able to think critically. Exacerbating all of this, discipline at the high school level is often confused with punishment, as zero-tolerance policies abound. Rather than teaching students alternatives to dealing with anger that do not include violence, too often secondary schools consider suspension or removal to an alternative campus when students make poor behavior choices.

HIGH SCHOOL BULLYING

As students grow older it becomes more difficult to arrive at a clear picture of their bullying experiences. In fact, some high school students report that bullying actually makes them strong and that they do not consider it a particularly serious problem. Older students are less likely to report bullying behaviors, and at the same time, they are less willing to admit to unhappiness. Some studies have also found that there is a tendency for people to err on the positive side when describing themselves. At the same time, high school students also tend to avoid people and places where bullying occurs, thus decreasing the chances of becoming a victim. Still, high school students in general, and bullying victims in particular, feel that school staff respond poorly to the bullying problems at their schools.

Typically, most studies have found anywhere from 14 percent to 34 percent of high school students report being bullied at least "sometimes," while 7 percent to 17 percent admit to bullying others. Bullying at the high school is most likely to occur in a school recreation area, in the classroom, in school hallways, and on the way home. Among high school students, the degree of physical and psychological bullying experienced can often predict how satisfied or dissatisfied students are with school. In fact, there is even some suggestion that physical peer abuse can lead to lower ACT/SAT scores.

High school students are most likely to bully other students because they do not fit in. Boys tend to select victims by their physical weakness, their short tempers, who their friends are, or their clothing. Girls, on the other hand, choose victims based on looks, emotionalism, weight, or who gets good grades. On the basis of studies by Borg (1999), Glover et al. (2000), Hazler (1996), Salmon (1998), Limber et al. (1998), Nansel et al. (2001), Olweus (1993), Rigby (1996), Shakeshaft et al. (1995), and others, this is some of what we know about the victims of bullying in the high school:

- Victims are just as likely to suffer name calling and stealing as younger victims.
- Victims are less likely to be hit or kicked, threatened, excluded, or lied about than younger victims.
- Victims tend to have more positive attitudes toward schoolwork than bullies.
- Victims believe that a common reason for being bullied is having good grades.

- Victims are more anxious than their high school peers.
- Victims are more likely to be viewed as lying about the bullying incident than the bullies.
- The number of victims decreases considerably at the high school level.
- Male victims are more likely to be victims of direct bullying than females.
- Male victims are often viewed as not "macho," unathletic, or "artsy."
- Female victims continue to report more indirect bullying, such as exclusion.
- Female victims are often seen by others as unattractive.
- Victims are likely to be targeted for atypical gender behaviors or racism.
- Victims have poorer relationships with classmates and are more lonely than bullies, more so for boys than girls.

Olweus (1993) has found that while the number of victims decreases at the high school level, the number of students who admit to bullying remains stable and that the percentage of boy bullies remains stable at all grade levels. Yet high school girls bully somewhat less than girls at other ages. While bullied students exhibit some of the same characteristics as their victims, there are some definite factors that set bullies apart from their victims. Based on the cited research, this is some of what we know about high school bullies:

- Bullies are more likely to resort to name calling and threatening than are bullies at other ages.
- Bullies are less likely to hit or kick, exclude others, and talk about others than younger bullies.
- Bullies are more likely to be depressed than their victims.
- Bullies hold higher social status than victims.
- Bullies tend to be more apt to use alcohol and tobacco.
- Bullies tend to have poorer academic achievement and perceive a poorer school climate.
- Seventy percent of high school bullies in an English study were found to have racist attitudes

- In the United States, black students are more likely than white or Hispanic students to report being called hate words.
- Female bullies are usually the same age as their victims.
- Male bullies are typically but not necessarily the same age as their victims.
- Male bullies are four times more likely to use direct bullying than girls.
- Male bullies are nearly as likely as female bullies to spread rumors about others.
- Male bullies are more likely to steal or damage others' property, while female bullies are less likely to break personal belongings but more likely to damage school property.

Bully/victims are young people who may have been seriously abused as children and seek to bully others. Indeed, domestic violence studies indicate that the abused are more likely than others to become abusers when they have their own families. Relatedly, Rigby (1996) reported a study where high school boys who had suffered bullying often were considerably more likely to be supportive of men who abused their wives. At the same time, one study of high-school-aged students found that as many as 35 percent reported being victims and bullies as well at least once within the past year (Borg 1999). Here are some characteristics of bully/victims, based primarily on studies of high school students:

- Bully/victims demonstrate a need to retaliate following acts of aggression.
- Female bully/victims strike back less than males.
- Bully/victims are involved more in smoking and drinking than other high school students.
- Bully/victims exhibit poorer academic achievement than victims.
- Bully/victims experience poorer relationships with classmates and increased loneliness compared with bullies.
- Bully/victims have parents with more permissive attitudes toward teen drinking; this is especially so for boys.

Bystanders at the high school level have a multitude of emotional responses to bullying. Some find it frightening, some ignore it completely, some consider it funny, while others are saddened by it. Regarding by-standers at the high school level, this is some of what we know about how bullying affects bystanders:

- Bystanders often feel anger and helplessness.
- Bystanders report nightmares and increased worry and fear.
- Bystanders often exaggerate reports of bullying in an effort to jus-tify their having failed to help the victim.
- Bystanders often do not become involved because they do not know how to respond.
- Bystanders generally experience a loss of self-respect.

LONG-TERM EFFECTS OF BULLYING

There is no doubt that bullying experiences have a multitude of nega-tive effects on the bully, the victim, and the bystander. Studies report that high school students feel that bullying has seriously impacted their physical, social, and academic well-being. Olweus (1993) followed seventy-one males who had been bully/victims during high school and found that even several years after graduation they had significantly more depression and poorer self-esteem than did their peers who had not been bullied. Another study followed for twenty-two years a group of third-grade students identified as highly aggressive. By age thirty, 25 percent of these individuals already had criminal records, compared with only 5 percent of other children (Eron et al. 1987). While very lit-tle long-term research involving girls has been done, Artz (1998) re-ported that girls who exhibit violent behavior often report higher rates of victimization, including bullying attacks by peers.

Bullying experiences cause students to feel less connected with the high school itself, which often leads to poor physical health, lowered participation in extracurricular events, violence, substance use, and even suicide. The ability to form natural relationships is often impaired, and some individuals even blame bullying for an inability to interact with the opposite sex. Additionally, many feel that this type of peer victimization and rejection by peers is a strong predictor of emotional disturbances in adulthood.

WHAT OUR HIGH SCHOOL BULLYING STUDY FOUND

We surveyed 136 ninth graders at two suburban high schools in Texas (see Harris, Petrie, and Willoughby 2002); a colleague, Jody Isernhagen, from the University of Nebraska–Lincoln, surveyed 115 ninth and tenth graders at two rural high schools in Nebraska (Harris and Isernhagen, at press; Isernhagen and Harris, at press). The Texas schools included Anglo, Hispanic, and black students, while the Nebraska students were almost completely Anglo. In the four schools, 110 students were boys and 140 were girls. Despite the differences between the two schools in Texas and the two schools in Nebraska, our findings were very similar.

How Often Does Bullying Happen at Your School?

Sixty-four percent of the students reported that bullying happened sometimes, and 18 percent indicated that it happened often. In other words, 72 percent of these students saw bullying happen at least "sometimes" on their school campus. However, just as in other studies, there is a discrepancy between high school students who reported seeing bullying happen and those who admitted that they themselves had been bullied. Thus, 40 percent reported that they had been bullied during the past year. At the same time, only 15 percent of the responding Texas ninth graders admitted that they did not "feel very safe" at school, while only 4 percent of the Nebraska students felt that way.

Where or When Does Bullying Happen?

The three places high school boys and girls most commonly indicated that bullying occurred at least "sometimes" were in class (78 percent), at lunch (75 percent), and at extracurricular events (66 percent), followed by on the way home from school (51 percent), during class breaks (46 percent), and on the way to school (27 percent).

What Kinds of Bullying Do High School Students Experience?

The majority of high school students reported that they were "at least" sometimes called names (45 percent), teased unpleasantly (44 percent), excluded from activities (31 percent), hit or kicked (24 percent), or threatened (20 percent). Considerably more boys than girls reported being threatened and hit or kicked.

How Do High School Students Feel after They Have Been Bullied?

Ten percent of the girls and 5 percent of the boys said that bullying made them feel miserable, while 15 percent of boys and 16 percent of girls reported that bullying made them feel angry. We were surprised at how many girls reported anger, since most research indicates that girls are most apt to feel sad or miserable. Regarding absences, less than 5 percent of students admitted to staying home from school because of bullying; however, nearly 25 percent had considered it at some time.

Whom Do High School Students Tell about Bullying?

Nearly twice as many girls as boys tell about being bullied; however, less than 20 percent of students tell anyone when they experience bullying or when they see it happening. When students do tell someone, they are most likely to tell their mother or a friend. However, less than 1 percent of high school students tell a teacher, counselor, or school administrator. Part of the reason students do not tell is the fear that bullying will become worse; 5 percent of boys and girls indicated that when these authorities were told, the bullying did in fact become worse. Students also decline to tell because they do not believe it will make any difference; in our study, 11 percent of boys and 17 percent of girls admitted to telling but reported that it made no difference.

CONCLUSION

Clearly, the findings of our study are consistent with the research that we have reported—bullying is a problem at the high school level. Additionally, our high school study reported findings that indicated that less than half of students believe that teachers and administrators are even interested in reducing bullying incidents at their schools, a finding consistent with other studies.

REFERENCES

Artz, S. (1998). *Sex, power, and the violent school girl.* Toronto: Trifolium Books.

Booth, W., and D. Snyder (2001). No remorse, no motive from shooting suspect. *San Antonio Express-News,* March 7, A1, A6.

Borg, M. (1999). The extent and nature of bullying among primary and secondary schoolchildren. *Educational Research* 41(2), 137–53.

Eron, L., et al. (1987). Aggression and its correlates over 22 years. In D. H. Crowell, I. M. Evans, and C. R. O'Donnell (eds.), *Childhood aggression and violence.* New York: Plenum.

"Fifty years to life for school shooting." (2002). *CBS News,* August 15, at www.cbsnews.com/stories/2002/08/15/national/main518874.shtml.

Glover, D., et al. (2000). Bullying in 25 secondary schools: Incidence, impact and intervention. *Educational Research* 42(2), 141–56.

Harris, S., and J. Isernhagen (at press). Bullying in Texas and Nebraska: A study of 9th graders. *Journal of at Risk Issues.*

Harris, S., G. Petrie, and W. Willoughby (2002). Bullying among 9th graders: An exploratory study. *NASSP Bulletin* 86(630), 3–14.

Hazler, R. (1996). Bystanders: An overlooked factor in peer on peer abuse. *Journal for the Professional Counselor* 11(2), 11–20.

Isernhagen, J., and S. Harris (at press). A comparison of 9th grade boys and girls bullying behaviors in Texas and Nebraska. *Journal of School Violence.*

Limber, S., et al. (1998). In M. Watts (ed.), *Cross-cultural perspectives on youth and violence: Contemporary studies in sociology,* vol. 18. Stamford, Conn.: Jai Press.

Nansel, T., et al. (2001). Bullying behaviors among U.S. youth: Prevalence and association with psychosocial adjustment. *Journal of American Medical Association* 285(16), 2094–2100.

Olweus, D. (1993). *Bullying at school.* Cambridge, Mass.: Blackwell.

Rigby, K. (1996). *Bullying in schools: And what to do about it.* London: Jessica Kingsley.

Salmon, G. (1998). Bullying in schools: Self reported anxiety, depression, and self esteem in secondary school children. *British Medical Journal* 317, 924–25.

Shakeshaft, C., et al. (1995). Peer harassment in schools. *Journal for a Just and Caring Education* 1(1), 30–44.

"Teen pleads guilty in school shooting." (2002). *San Antonio Express-News*, June 21, 1.

Violent kids: Can we change the trend? (2000). New York: National Issues Forums Institute and Public Agenda. Kettering Foundation.

7

HIGH SCHOOL BULLYING PREVENTIONS AND INTERVENTIONS

*Jordan Prinzi knows bullying when he sees it, and the 16-year-old be-
lieves there's one way to stop it. "At some point, you're going to
fight," the high school junior says. "There's no rule that can stop it.
If it gets bad enough, guys are going to go at it" (Bowles 2001, 4A)*

*Colin Ferguson will admit to deliberately staying away from
school, saying he knew what awaited him in class. "I was going to
face hatred," said Ferguson, a 16-year-old student . . . who is gay.
Often taunted[,] . . . Ferguson said he won't forget the day last October when a classmate told him "fags are going to hell." After that,
the male classmate threatened to beat him up after school (Hewitt
2002, 21A)*

Breaking ranks: Changing an American institution (1996), a report of
the National Association of Secondary School Principals in partnership
with the Carnegie Foundation, challenged U.S. high schools to reevalu-
ate their purpose and functions: "A young person who grows into adulthood unequipped to reach his or her full potential will possess neither
the knowledge nor the will to contribute to making this a better society"
(p. 4). The report pointed out that nearly one-third of children under
the age of eighteen no longer live with both parents, that 20 percent of
our children are raised in poverty, that tens of thousands of high school

students become parents themselves every year, and that without education, the only jobs available continue the cycle of poverty.

A key initiative in *Breaking Ranks* encouraged high schools to emphasize personalization, by limiting high schools to no more than six hundred students. The purpose of this proposal was to enhance relationships among students and teachers and also allow a variety of instructional strategies to accommodate better the needs of individual students. Another area of emphasis was the need to build "an understanding of and respect for diversity[,] . . . to equip students for the interdependency of life in the 21st century" (p. 68). As we move into the new millennium, the challenge of this report is even more necessary considering the effects of our global community and the need to get along with others.

Certainly, today's secondary academic climate is marked by many responsibilities, including that of students to pass state-mandated tests and to accumulate credentials that will allow them to be accepted into the right colleges. Yet it is especially critical for high schools to find time to address the personal, relational needs of students. At the same time, most programs that address the need for students to develop an understanding of others and the ability to get along with others, programs that include intervention in and prevention of bullying, also have a positive influence on related inappropriate behaviors that plague secondary students, such as drug abuse, truancy, dropping out of school, and poor academic performance.

However, bullying at the high school level is much more difficult to identify, due to the subtleties of student-to-student and teacher relationships, than it is with younger children. High school students rarely report bullying behavior; have more physical, unsupervised freedom on the school campus; and have learned to use bullying behaviors covertly, rather than openly. Thus, in addition to becoming more relational, high school faculty must be trained to look for all forms of intimidation.

CREATING A CLIMATE THAT IS AFFIRMING AND SAFE

Educators across the nation have resorted to many strategies in an effort to make the school day safer for children. Some of these strategies include installing video cameras in difficult-to-supervise areas, requiring anyone who enters the building to go through electronic screening, increasing supervision by faculty, and hiring police. Educators have also made schools safer by implementing policies that require visitors to sign in and out at the school office and having faculty and visitors wear identity badges. Safety drills and practice "lockdowns" are conducted for use in emergencies. Other schools, such as Patterson High School in Baltimore, Maryland, have been organized into smaller, self-contained units that focus on transitioning ninth graders and into "career academies" for upper-level students (McPartland et al. 1997).

However, for most teenagers the climate of the school is generally a reflection of how students feel about the school; its effect on learning can be tremendous. For example, students who fear being bullied, teased, or taunted, who are frustrated, lonely, or misunderstood, or have other negative feelings are likely to perform poorly socially, as well as academically. Conversely, students who feel secure, safe, accomplished, valued, supported, and have other positive feelings are likely to be positive in their understanding of the school and its activities.

Educational philosopher Jane Roland Martin (1992) suggests that while educators should continue to raise academic standards, they should also create a school climate that focuses on the "three Cs": care, concern, and connection. This means that students must be prepared to care for themselves and others, they must have concern for others, and they must have attitudes and skills needed to build relationships that connect them to others.

Developing a climate of tolerance for others must be an essential part of the high school curriculum, since many students are faced with painful incidents of bullying behavior, bullying that extends the traditional reasons and focuses on racial, religious, and sexual orientation differences. In fact, according to Jon Davidson, senior counsel for Lambda Legal Defense and Educational Fund, Inc., schools "can either try to prevent harassment before it happens, deal with it appropriately when it does, or they can face dealing with it later, perhaps in lawsuits" (Hewitt 2002, 22A). Davidson is currently representing a twenty-one-year-old man who has sued a Nevada school district and a teacher because nothing was done to prevent harassment. The young man had endured "daily nightmares" of being taunted at school and spat upon while riding on the school bus.

As life becomes more global, we are confronted with examples of intolerance everywhere, almost on a daily basis, not just in our schools. One urban school in Connecticut involved students and faculty members in a study on prejudice. They attended sessions on communication, trust, prejudgment, self-image, and victimization, and participated in activities, group discussions, and role playing. When it was over, one student commented, "I got a better idea about how different people think. For example, when people get into a fight, they throw things in people's faces that they are the way they are because they are Asian, Black, White, or Puerto Rican. This helped me practice talking things over instead of being physical" (Richardson 1995, 40).

High schools that emphasize the following qualities create affirming school climates that nurture young people and prevent bullying behaviors:

Leadership. Involve students in the leadership and governance of the school—for example, having students be a part of site-based committees and strategic planning committees.

Responsibility. Encourage a feeling of responsibility for one another among students and faculty; this includes the responsibility to not interfere with the rights of others.

Communication. Encourage students and faculty to discuss openly issues of concern rather than remain silent.

Kindness. Emphasize the importance of simply treating others with respect, regardless of differences.

Collaboration. Encourage students to work with others and to value their differences, talents, and abilities rather than set apart or mock others due to race, sex, religion, size, etc.

Critical thinking. Encourage students to solve problems together when difficult issues occur, rather than immediately expect the school faculty to make all decisions. Critical thinking also encourages students to identify stereotyping that occurs at school, in the media, and elsewhere.

COMMUNICATING APPROPRIATE BEHAVIORAL STANDARDS TO HIGH SCHOOL STUDENTS

Even at the high school level, educators should never make the mistake of assuming that all students arrive at school already understanding that bullying behavior is inappropriate and how to react properly when these circumstances occur. The importance of clearly communicating to students what is expected is critical. Clear guidelines not only create a disciplined environment but also enhance a young person's understanding of right and wrong behaviors. Daniel Duke, in his book *Creating safe schools for all children* (2002), outlined several issues that should be considered when developing guidelines for behavior in school. These same issues can be considered when developing guidelines against bullying:

- What form will guidelines take? For example, will they be written as "thou shalt treat everyone with respect," or "thou shalt not bully?"
- What characteristics do the rules have? Good rules are reasonable, nondiscriminatory, clear, and consistent.
- What behaviors do rules need to address? Identify the specific behaviors in the definition. For example: Bullying includes harmful teasing, taunting, threatening, intentionally excluding others, spreading rumors, stealing, and physically abusing others.
- Which rules can cause confusion? Bullying often causes confusion because of other terms associated with it, such as harassment and hazing. These terms should be defined in school guidelines.
- Who should make the rules? Students and parents should be encouraged to give input into the rules, but how much input is enough?
- How should rules be shared with students? What has the faculty done to ensure that students understand the meaning of bullying and why it is inappropriate behavior?

Cypress-Fairbanks Independent School District (2001–2002), a recognized school district in northwestern Houston, Texas, provides each student with a "discipline management plan" and "student code of conduct." The code begins with a list of student expectations, which include "demonstrate courtesy and respect for others," "respect the rights and privileges of other students," "respect the property of others," and "report dangerous behaviors and or situations to school personnel" (CC-2). Misbehaviors are listed as levels of violations (I, II, and III) with corresponding disciplinary options. For example, "verbally or physically taunting or bullying other students" is listed as a Level II violation; disciplinary options (of which one or more may be used) include a student conference with parent, teacher, counselor, or administrator; community service assignment; detention hall; exclusion from extracurricular activities; and in-school suspension.

An important component of any disciplinary management plan is that consequences be considered in both negative and positive ways. While punishment or negative reinforcement, such as the assignment of after-school detention hall, can be an appropriate form of consequence for misbehavior, there are times when positive reinforcement, which is most commonly used to strengthen or maintain a behavior, is important.

HELPING STUDENTS LEARN POSITIVE INTERPERSONAL SKILLS

Adult awareness of the importance of being a good role model is a key ingredient in helping students learn positive interpersonal skills. This takes place informally, as a natural part of the school day. Yet there are also many ways in which high schools formally focus on teaching positive interpersonal skills; these include requiring students to participate in community service, establishing mentor programs, training students in conflict resolution skills, and teaching a curriculum that emphasizes moral or character education.

Encouraging students to become connected to the community through service learning offers an excellent opportunity to learn positive interpersonal skills as well as encourage empathy. There are many ways to involve students in community projects, such as visiting nursing homes, displaying artwork on the walls of local businesses, and tutoring younger students. While in some schools this is voluntary, more and more high schools are requiring students to be involved in service learning projects before they graduate.

In recent years, the importance of mentor programs has grown. Mentor programs involve partnering a faculty member with a student and then providing time for the two to build a relationship. In some cases, mentor programs have extended this partnership to the local community; businesses "adopt" students to mentor. Another way to create a mentor program is for schools to pair older students with younger students to build a supportive relationship at school. An example of a peer mentor program is the Natural Helpers program, which promotes the idea that it is okay to seek help from classmates and from adults. This peer-helping program involves school counselors and teachers training and supporting students, who then help other students by listening, providing information, and referring them to appropriate resources within the community.

Moral education is generally thought of within a structured curriculum, under the rubric of "character education." However, at the high school level, many other opportunities exist to use current local, national, and world events to discuss moral issues that are a part of our everyday lives. For example, R. E. Myers (2001) tells about a teacher who wrote a story for a high school class to discuss concerning the problem of violence at school. Using the following problem solving format, students were asked to:

- Identify the problem
- List different ways to solve the problem
- List what they knew about possible solutions
- Weigh advantages and disadvantages of possible solutions
- Indicate what might happen if they tried a possible solution
- Discuss whether they should try another solution
- Share what they had learned

Teaching students the meaning of values and the importance of making wise choices is a valuable component of character education programs. The resource list at the end of this chapter includes character education programs that are appropriate for high school students.

Conflict is a natural part of any day; therefore, it comes as no surprise that conflict is a natural part of the high school day. Yet for optimum learning to occur, students must learn how to deal with conflict in appropriate ways. One way to do this is through peer-mediation or conflict-resolution strategies. According to David and Roger Johnson (1995), the best school programs in conflict resolution tend to follow six key principles:

Go Beyond Violence Prevention to Conflict Resolution Training. Too often violence prevention programs are unsuccessful because they do not teach young people how to deal with conflict appropriately.

Don't Attempt to Eliminate All Conflicts. Appropriate conflict can increase achievement, motivation, and even healthy development; conflict becomes inappropriate when it becomes destructive.

Create a Cooperative Context. Ideal conflict resolution programs attempt to transform the total school environment into a nonviolent learning community.

Decrease In-School Risk Factors. These factors—which include academic failure, alienation, and psychological pathology—can be reduced by emphasizing cooperative learning, by encouraging supportive peer relationships, and by teaching young people how to work cooperatively with others.

Use Academic Controversy to Increase Learning. Academic controversy exists when the ideas of one student are incompatible with those of another, but the two seek to reach an agreement. Teaching students strategies (such as assigned sides to debate) that view the issue from both perspectives encourages consensus.

Teach All Students How to Resolve Conflicts Constructively. The total student body, not just a cadre, should be taught skills in conflict resolution, negotiation, and mediation.

RESOURCES TO PREVENT/REDUCE BULLYING

A list of resources to prevent or reduce bullying at the high school level is listed below. Use this list as a place to begin; many other excellent resources are available.

School Curricula

Community service for teens series. (1998). Ferguson. This is a series of eight titles, each approximately ninety-four pages, written specifically for teenagers in grades nine to twelve. Each book focuses on a different area of service, that includes caring for animals, helping the ill, the poor, the elderly, neighborhood service, protecting the environment, promoting the arts and sciences, participating in government, and serving with the police, fire, and EMS.

Conflict resolution: A curriculum for youth providers. National Resource Center for Youth Services, University of Oklahoma, Tulsa, (918) 585-2986, www.nrcys.ou.edu/default.htm. Designed for secondary schools. Its key elements include helping students define conflict, teaching three types of conflict resolution, and reviewing basic communications behavior.

Healing the hate: A national hate crime prevention curriculum. National Hate Crime Prevention Project, Education Development Center, Inc., 55 Chapel Street, Newton, MA, (800) 225-4276. This program, designed for middle and high school students, teaches about violence and prejudice. It emphasizes developing empathy, critical thinking, and perspective.

King, L., ed. (2000). *Hear my voice: A multicultural anthology of literature from the United States.* Addison-Wesley. This collection of stories, poems, essays, and speeches, celebrates diversity and explores issues relating to conflict, personal identity, and other life issues. A teacher's guide is included.

Peer Culture Development (PCD). Contact: Todd Hoover, School of Education, MC Campus, Loyola University, 1041 Ridge Road, Wilmette, IL 60091, (847) 853-3320. This program for junior and high schools is run by counselors as a for-credit class for at-risk students. The program assumes that self-confidence may be gained by being of service to others and that adolescents who have learned to solve their own problems can help others.

Resolving Conflict Creatively Program (RCCP). Contact: RCCP National Center, 40 Exchange Place, Suite 1111, New York, NY 10005, (212) 509-0022. This program is designed for grades K–12 to cultivate emotional, social, and ethical development in young people through teaching concepts and skills in conflict resolution and intergroup relations.

The School Safety Program. Contact: Dennis Kenney, Director of Research, Police Executive Research Forum, 1120 Connecticut Avenue NW, Suite 030, Washington, DC 20036, (202) 466-7820. The focus of this program is to identify violence problems and devise effective responses.

Just for High School Students

Perry, S. (2000). *Catch the spirit: Teen volunteers tell how they made a difference.* Franklin Watts. Created for grades nine to twelve by the Prudential Insurance Company of America and the National Association of Secondary School Principals. This book tells inspirational stories of twenty teen volunteers who have worked in a variety of programs and motivated others to also do so.

Service learning series. (2000). Children's Press/Grolier. This is a series of six books that feature service learning for grades six to ten. It includes directions for implementing service-learning projects related to community and also volunteer opportunities with children, senior citizens, and animals.

Just for Parents

Espeland, P., and E. Verdick. (1998). *Making every day count: Daily readings for young people on solving problems, setting goals and feeling good about yourself.* Free Spirit. This handbook for teenagers provides daily readings featuring inspirational quotes and essays expanding each quote.

Salt, J. S. (1999). *Always accept me for who I am: Instructions from teenagers on raising the perfect parent.* Random House. This book is a collection of parenting tips from teenagers thirteen to eighteen years old.

Wiley, L. (1998). *Building activities: For high school and college classes.* Character Development Foundation, (603) 472-3063. Designed for grades nine to twelve, this collection of activities promotes a positive classroom community by teaching respect, affirming and caring about each other, and building membership within a group.

Videos

In search of character. (1999). Video Series. Live Wire Media, (800) 359-KIDS. Grades six to twelve. This is a series of ten videocassettes that focuses on core character traits, such as trustworthiness, respect, responsibility, fairness, caring, etc. Profiles feature teens who exemplify good character and guide discussion.

Names can really hurt us. Anti-Defamation League Materials Library, 22-D Hollywood Ave., Hohokus, NJ 07423, (800) 343-5540. This is a series of vignettes in which high school students describe hurtful incidents of prejudice and discrimination.

The truth about hate. (1999). AIMS, (800) 367-2467. Created for grades eight to twelve, this video addresses the issues of respect, tolerance, and kindness through the eyes of teenagers.

Websites

Centers for Disease Control and Prevention, Division of Violence Prevention, www.cdc.gov/ncipc/dvp/dvp.htm. This division has four priority areas for violence prevention: youth violence, family and intimate violence, suicide, and firearm injuries.

Community of Caring, www.communityofcaring.org. Founded by the Joseph P. Kennedy Foundation, COC addresses destructive attitudes that lead to dropping out of school.

Ethics Resource Center, www.ethics.org. This center has a character education program that includes a character calendar, links to other resources, and books on moral development.

Institute for Global Ethics, www.globalethics.org. Monthly ethical dilemmas test one's "ethical fitness."

Justice Information Center, www.ncjrs.org. The National Criminal Justice Reference Service (NCJRS) is an extensive source of information on criminal and juvenile justice, providing services to an international community of policy makers and professionals.

Partnerships against Violence Network, www.pavnet.org/. This is a library of information about violence and youth at risk, including data from seven federal agencies.

REFERENCES

Bowles, S. (2001). Educators try to establish anti-bully policies. *USA Today*, April 17, 4A.

Cypress-Fairbanks Independent School District (2001–2002). *Student handbook & Code of Conduct 2001–2001.* Houston, Tex.: Cypress-Fairbanks ISD.

Duke, D. (2002). *Creating safe schools for all children.* Boston: Allyn & Bacon.

Hewitt, P. (2002). Seeking tolerance: Gay teens, educators discuss harassment issues. *Houston Chronicle,* April 4, 21A.

Johnson, D., and R. Johnson (1995). Why violence prevention programs don't work—and what does. *Educational Leadership* 52(5), at www.ascd.org/readingroom/edlead/9502/johnson.html (accessed January 16, 2002).

Martin, J. R. (1992). *The Schoolhome.* Cambridge, Mass.: Harvard University Press.

McPartland, J., et al. (1997). Finding safety in small numbers. *Educational Leadership* 55(2), 14–17.

Myers, R. E. (2001). Taking a common-sense approach to moral education. *The Clearing House* 74(4), 219–20.

National Association of Secondary School Principals (1996). *Breaking ranks: Changing an American institution.* Reston, Va.: National Association of Secondary School Principals.

Richardson, A. (1995). Teaching tolerance to middle school students. *Schools in the Middle* 5(2), 39–40.

HOW ADULTS CAN SUPPORT A BULLY-FREE ENVIRONMENT

Until recently, Daniel, 8 years old, came home from school almost every day complaining that he had been tripped and pushed around by a classmate during recess. It wasn't until his mother brought the situation to the attention of one of Danny's teachers that the bullying stopped (Ross-Toren 2001, C-1).

In 9th grade I was the victim of pervasive, severe racial and sexual harassment. I was incessantly called names such as "whore" and "slut." Vulgar songs were sung openly about me during classes. My home was vandalized repeatedly. Teachers and school officials did little to help me. When I told one school official about my classmates' . . . plans to pool their lunch money to buy a rifle to shoot me, he suggested that my problems would end if I would only be more submissive, "like the other girls." After realizing that school officials were unwilling to help protect me, I was forced to transfer to another high school.

—Erika Harold, who became Miss America 2003, on September 21, 2002 (Harold 2002, 13A)

FAMILY ISSUES IN BULLYING

While we know that there are many factors that contribute to violence, we also believe that violence is largely a learned behavior, and that learning occurs in many settings, beginning in the home. Rigby (1996) suggests that long before they go to school, within the first few years of life children develop ways of behaving and reacting to events, and this affects how they relate to others at school. Certainly, bullying behavior often manifests itself within the school day and related school activities, but the family and its relationship to bullying must be considered. Our focus in this chapter is not to place blame on the family or with the school but to examine the issue of bullies and their victims in the larger context of the family. We do not want to stereotype families of bullies and victims, but it is important to note some of the often shared characteristics of both groups.

Family Circumstances of Bullies

According to Rigby (1996), even in the earliest years of schooling, children who bully others tend to:

- Be bigger and stronger than others (especially boys)
- Be aggressive
- Be impulsive
- Exhibit little empathy for others
- Not be very cooperative

If there are parents who still view bullying as a "kids will be kids" behavior, there are also parents who actually encourage bullying behavior, by encouraging children to "stand up for themselves" without any adult support. Generally, though, according to Hoover and Oliver (1996), several factors often characterize the family lives of bullies; they live in emotionally charged environments that are sometimes cold and disconnected, and sometimes heavy with anger. Olweus (1980, 1984) identified four factors within the home environment that were found to be related to aggression: negativism, especially by the mother; neglect and rejection by those responsible for caring for the child; treating aggression with permissiveness; and harsh child-rearing practices. Likewise, Eron (1987) found that the best predictors of future aggressive behavior were being rejected by a parent, receiving physical punishment often, not being nurtured, and living in a home with parental disharmony.

Rigby (1996, p. 74) reported that boy and girl bullies described their families in some of the following ways:

- My family does not sympathize with me and understand when I feel sad.
- Members of my family are not encouraged to work together in dealing with family problems.
- My father does not care about me or accept the sort of person I am.
- Honesty is not important in our family.
- We do not feel free to express our opinions in our family.
- We do not consider each other's feelings.

At the same time, the pattern of abuse appears to be cyclical. In other words, adults who have been bullies as children tend to have children who are bullies. As adults, these former childhood bullies are also more likely to be involved with violent crime and spousal abuse, and frequently to resort to severe punishment with their own children—and the dysfunction continues.

Family Circumstances of Victims

Even when children begin school, those who are more frequently victimized often (Rigby 1996):

- Are physically less strong than others (particularly so with boys)
- Are timid
- Are introverted
- Have low self-esteem
- Have few friends

There is not as clear a picture of the family life of the victim as exists for the bully. Yet family relationships among victim families appear to have some similarities to those of bullies; these include relationship difficulties between parent and child, disharmony in the home, family financial problems, and relationship problems outside the home (Olweus 1980). However, one major difference is that victims, or "whipping boys" (as

Olweus called them), often live in families that respond too emotionally to their child's victimization (Hoover and Oliver 1996).

Further, victims tend to be sensitive, passive, and very dependent on parents, who are in turn often overprotective. Consequently, these children often tend to be more comfortable with adults than they are with children of their own age. Additionally, they fail to develop strategies to build basic relationships with other children, let alone strategies to deal with bullies.

SCHOOL PERSONNEL ATTITUDES TOWARD BULLYING AND VICTIMS

Certainly, like some parents, there are teachers who feel that bullying is just a natural part of growing up and that children should learn to stand up for themselves. Others simply fail to acknowledge that bullying happens on their campuses. When we first became interested in researching the problem of bullying, we visited a school administrator in a community where the problem of bullying was so severe that the local newspaper had carried several articles about it within district schools. Yet, and despite the claims of students, the administrator insisted that the newspapers were exaggerating, that bullying was not a problem within the district's schools.

Still, more and more educators are willing to acknowledge that bullying at school is a problem and want to see something done. They do not feel that bullying is inevitable; they definitely believe that something can be done to reduce or even stop bullying in their schools. For example, Rigby (1996) reported that when teachers and students were asked the same questions about bullying, the teachers were even more supportive of the victim and anti-bully than the students. Almost unanimously, teachers believed that children should report if they were being bullied, while only one-third of the students thought that they should report being bullied. Nearly all of the teachers felt that students who were harassed did not deserve this treatment; half of the students thought they did deserve it or were not sure.

Yet Rigby (1996) has reported that when teachers were asked if they felt that they could act effectively to stop bullying, one-third admitted to being intimidated by bullies and felt that someone else (usually the principal) should deal with this situation, not classroom teachers. Further highlighting the gap between what teachers believe about bullying and how supportive students see their behavior is the fact that nearly one-third of students saw teachers as either "not interested" or "only sometimes interested" in stopping bullying.

Our colleague Jody Isernhagen reports that nearly 90 percent of 141 Nebraska teachers surveyed responded that teachers at their school were at least "usually" interested in trying to stop bullying. Yet only 56 percent of students felt that teachers were interested in trying to stop bullying, 30 percent of students indicated they did not know if teachers were interested or not, and nearly 12 percent of students said that teachers were not. In our study of bullying in Texas among ninth graders, only 25 percent of students felt that administrators were interested in reducing bullying, and only 31 percent thought that teachers were interested.

Clearly, there exists a disconnect between what school personnel believe about the severity of bullying—necessary knowledge to combat these behaviors—and how students perceive the concern of teachers and administrators. Therefore, discussing bullying in staff development, providing classroom teachers and other personnel with appropriate strategies that work in reducing bullying, and beginning a dialogue between students and faculty are all critical to the success of any school.

WHY VICTIMS AND BYSTANDERS RARELY TELL ADULTS ABOUT BULLYING

Victims rarely tell that they are being bullied for a variety of reasons, such as fear, not knowing how to express themselves, and also because no one wants to be a "tattletale." Bystanders rarely tell anyone about the bullying they observe, for the very same reasons. Thus, it is not uncommon in schools, as well as in families, for a "code of silence" to exist. Frequently children do not tell adults about being bullied or having seen bullying occur, because they feel that neither parents nor the school will deal with the problem appropriately. In fact, if reports are not dealt with properly and anonymously, students could experience more severe physical and emotional suffering. This is why it is important for children to have a safe way to report these events.

Sometimes victims, as well as bystanders, do not report bullying because adults are "indifferent listeners" (Ross 1996, p. 95), who expect children to be able to handle their own problems and stand up for themselves. Other times, students do not tell simply because they are embarrassed to find themselves unable to handle a problem such as this. Unfortunately, sometimes children who have been chronically bullied actually begin to feel that they somehow deserve being treated this way.

HOW PARENTS AND SCHOOL PERSONNEL CAN WORK TOGETHER TO REDUCE BULLYING

How Parents Can Help When Their Child Is a Bully

The home is the first place to begin working with children to prevent bullying behaviors. Certainly, to love children, demonstrate affection toward them, and help them form strong core values that emphasize kindness and cooperation are critical. Strategies to guide parents in helping their own children not become bullies include:

- Using teachable moments with siblings and other children to reinforce the importance of kindness and cooperation
- Teaching children to care for pets
- Openly sharing with children how important they are
- Reflecting on a parent's own upbringing and attempts to resolve their own anger, bitterness, and other destructive behaviors
- Participating in a parenting program through the school, church, or other community agency
- Building self-esteem in children by affirming their value and worth
- Teaching children to deal with anger appropriately by role-modeling positive anger management
- Teaching about empathy through the use of role playing—for example, encouraging children to role-play what happened and how they felt, then asking them to role-play the other individual's part
- Helping children become comfortable with individual differences

How Parents Can Help When Their Child Is a Victim

There are strategies for a parent to follow at home that can help a victimized child respond to bullying. They include:

- Helping children who are being bullied to not blame themselves
- Sharing their own experiences with the children
- Building a child's self-esteem with positive, affirming actions
- Helping a child manage often repressed anger at being a victim
- Emphasizing the importance of having told the parent

It is also important for parents to discuss protective strategies for victims, to include ignoring the behavior, undergoing assertiveness training, using humor, recommending the use of alternate routes, and encouraging them not to be afraid to call out for help.

Parents in Cooperation with Teachers and School Administrators

A key component in reducing bullying is for parents to inform the school immediately when their child has become a victim. When parents and school personnel work together, the victimized child can best be supported; help for the bully can also result. When the school contacts parents with the concern that their child is bullying others or even being bullied, often a parent's first tendency is to blame the school. But it is vital that parents listen, then gather as much information as they can about how their child is doing socially and academically at school. Working in partnership with the school, parents can direct their child's behavior in positive ways to build relationships with other children. If a child continues to bully others, it is likely a symptom of an underlying problem, and professional counseling should be considered. If a child continues to be victimized, professional counseling should also be sought.

There are several strategies for parents and school personnel, working together, to consider in order to reduce bullying behaviors. One strategy is openly to discuss bullying at home and at school, conveying that it is inappropriate behavior that is harmful to the victim, bystanders, and ultimately, the bully. When adults engage children in this type of discussion, they reinforce the idea that everyone has a responsibility to each other and that reporting incidents of harmful bullying is important. When parents and the school know that bullying is occurring, they are able to support victims, bystanders, and bullies and thus reduce bullying at school. A key component, therefore, is informing the school immediately. Other strategies for parents and school personnel include:

- Parents communicating with the school with an attitude of cooperation
- School personnel viewing parents as partners
- Concerned parents making appointments with appropriate school personnel, rather than arriving at the office unannounced
- Working together to create a discipline-management plan for a bully to curtail inappropriate behaviors
- Working together to create a behavior plan to provide a victim with strategies to respond to bullying
- Involving school personnel and parents on a committee to develop policies against peer abuse

HOW THE COMMUNITY AND THE SCHOOL CAN WORK TOGETHER TO REDUCE BULLYING

Twelve states have enacted anti-bullying legislation: Oklahoma, Michigan, Colorado, Georgia, New Hampshire, Washington, Connecticut, Louisiana, West Virginia, Delaware, Pennsylvania, and Alaska. Three others are considering doing so: Illinois, Oregon, and New York. Their legislation orders school districts to create specific plans to reduce violence and make schools safer.

While much of the responsibility for addressing bullying falls squarely on the shoulders of the schools, communities have resources that can aid the fight against bullying. One particularly helpful option is to create a support group within the community, churches, or in the school for parents and students interested in reducing bullying. Other support groups can be created for victims of bullying, for example. A primary purpose of a support group is to reassure victims that they are not alone and that there is help available. In addition to providing emotional support, these groups are also valuable places to begin dialogue that can lead to changing behaviors and thus decrease a child's propensity for being bullied.

Rigby (1996) reports that Australia has established over ninety thousand Safety Houses, constituting a network of safe places for children endangered on the way to and from school for any reason, including bullying. In 1995, over 20 percent of incidents leading to the use of a Safety House involved bullying by peers. We are not aware of any Safe Houses in the United States; we would encourage communities to consider establishing such a network.

Some communities have also established anonymous telephone Kids Help Lines or Child Abuse Hotlines, staffed by trained counselors experienced in dealing with the problems of children. Community recreation centers, church activities, and community service organizations provide opportunities that often redirect children's behaviors and involve them in positive, affirming activities. In San Antonio, Texas, a free program called Great Start is a collaborative effort among four nonprofit groups to provide parental education to at-risk families where abuse or neglect is present. Another example is the Utah Center for Families in Education, which focuses on the needs of school-aged children and families; it is a cooperative program involving state officials, school personnel, families, and community members. Frequently businesses partner with schools to provide adult mentors for students. This is another excellent opportunity for children to build friendships with adults, which help develop positive relationship skills.

Building trusting relationships with adults is an important component in the effort to reduce bullying, and fortunately, this challenge is not isolated to one group of adults alone. The responsibility for reducing bullying behaviors in children is shared between the family, the school, and the larger community. When adults meet this challenge, they can not only change lives of children but have a positive impact on the entire community.

REFERENCES

Eron, L. (1987). Aggression through the ages. *School Safety,* Fall, 12–16.
Hamilton, A. (2002). Oklahoma passes anti-bullying law. *Dallas Morning News,* May 6, 1A.

Harold, E. (2002). Harassment causes long-term pain. *USA Today*, October 4, 13A.

Hoover, J., and R. Oliver (1996). *The bullying prevention handbook*. Bloomington, Ind.: National Education Service.

Olweus, D. (1980). Familial and temperamental determinants of aggressive behaviors in adolescent boys: A causal analysis. *Developmental Psychology* 16, 644–60.

———. (1984). Aggressors and their victims: Bullying in school. In N. Frude and H. Gault (eds.), *Disruptive behavior in schools*. New York: Wiley.

Rigby, K. (1996). *Bullying in schools and what to do about it*. London: Jessica Kingsley.

Ross, D. (1996). *Childhood bullying and teasing: What school personnel, other professionals, and parents can do*. Alexandria, Va.: American Counseling Association.

Ross-Toren, C. (2001). Today's childhood bully could become tomorrow's criminal. *San Antonio Express-News*, October 29, C-1.

9

CREATING SAFE SCHOOLS
FOR ALL STUDENTS

"We have to send the message that no one should go to school in fear."

—David Brooks, president of the Newport-Mesa Board of Education (Bowles 2001, 4A)

"Discrimination is not to be accepted in any of our schools."

—Laurie Bricker, Houston Independent School District board president (Hewitt 2002, A21)

"As Miss America 2003, I am issuing a national call to action, challenging all segments of American society to take a proactive, comprehensive approach to eradicating this culture of degradation and indifference. . . . Freeing our youth from harassment will empower them to become the change we seek in this world" (Harold 2002, 13A).

The challenge to reduce bullying behaviors at school is for all of us, whether we are educators, parents, students, or other community members. But adults bear the greatest responsibility to begin a discussion of bullying that recognizes it for what it is—a reprehensible act that devalues others. It is up to adults to demonstrate through actions how to live without bullying others. Our children are watching us, and they watch to see if we live the mantra of kindness and equality of opportunity for all of which we speak so easily—or whether we ignore bullying behaviors, close our eyes, and refuse to see the hurt in a child's eyes.

WARNING SIGNS THAT A CHILD IS BEING BULLIED

As we have stated earlier, too often children are not willing to report that they are being bullied to anyone. Occasionally victims tell a friend, but this rarely results in the needed support that telling a concerned adult should elicit. Sometimes, even though a child is reluctant to tell, there are warning signs that observant parents or school officials might notice. These might be physical, such as coming home from school or an activity with torn clothes or bruises, and an unwilling or suspect explanation. Occasionally, children who are being bullied have psychosomatic symptoms, such as stomach pains or headache and ask to stay home from school. Other warning signs are behavioral and include (Dawkins and Hill, as cited in Rigby 1996, p. 240):

- Fear of walking to or from school
- Changing route to or from school
- Asking to be taken to school
- Unwillingness to go to school
- Doing poorly on school work
- Coming home from school hungry (because lunch money was taken)
- Losing possessions
- Having few friends
- Not being invited to parties
- Becoming withdrawn
- Stammering
- Displaying temper outbursts
- Appearing upset, unhappy, stressed
- Losing appetite
- Appearing anxious: wetting bed, biting nails
- Losing sleep at night

- Refusing to say what is wrong
- Making poor excuses for any of the above behaviors

Once we recognize that bullying is happening on our school campuses, we can begin to provide the support that students need. The following section recaps what educators are doing to provide this support.

WHAT EDUCATORS ARE DOING

Clearly, the school is a major influence in the lives of children; after all, most children spend a minimum of 175 days a year and at least eight hours a day in school. Because successful challenges to reduce bullying involve the whole school climate, no one program or single activity can serve as a silver bullet. Consequently, school personnel are most likely to be successful in reducing and preventing bullying when they build caring cultures and integrate several areas of responsibility, including parent participation programs, school security procedures, programs for safe schools, and systemic changes within the schools.

Parent Participation Programs

At every grade level, educators are making efforts to increase the number of contacts between parents and school personnel. This is happening through parent involvement programs that allow parents opportunities to demonstrate support for their child's education in a variety of ways, such as learning how to tutor a child, encouraging completion of homework, and supporting the school's discipline policies. Parent support teams are created for parents to reach out to each other and encourage each other to involve themselves as decision makers in their children's academic lives, thus increasing opportunities for student success. Many schools are conducting home visits in this effort to improve relationships between schools and the parents.

School Security Procedures

Due to demands from legislators and communities, schools are doing more than ever before to establish and follow procedures designed to protect children. For example, Seattle Public Schools in 1997 had thirty-two bomb threats. The school system redesigned bomb-threat procedures in ways that included an improved education process and communication with administration and on-site staff; in 1999, only one call was received (Agron 1999). School personnel are also exploring available technology, from alarm systems to improved security camera systems. Almost without exception, all school personnel are reviewing and revising discipline policies to improve student and teacher safety at school (Harris and Harris 2001).

Programs for Safe Schools

From kindergarten through high school, educators are implementing strategies that focus on monitoring behavior, predicting risk, and intervening early. These programs include training for students and teachers that improves social competency skills and encourages critical thinking skills. Other programs focus on implementing conflict resolution and peer mediation to help students work through conflict appropriately. These programs are especially valuable in reducing bullying in that they create new patterns for interactions among students within the culture of the school day.

Many school district boards and administrators have adopted school curricula that focus on teaching character and moral development throughout the school day. Cooperative learning is an instructional format that encourages children in building positive relationships by interacting with other students in the classroom. Other school faculty have implemented before and after-school programs to provide activities for students under the supervision of adults. Mentoring programs, such as the Neighborhood Longhorns at the University of Texas, involve college students mentoring at-risk students. All of these programs interact in a variety of ways to reduce bullying behaviors and encourage social skills that build affirming peer relationships.

Systemic Changes within the School

How schools are structured has an effect on student achievement, attendance, and behavior. Charter schools, career academies, schools-within-schools, magnet schools, and alternative schools all represent efforts to build a sense of community among students. Efforts at school restructuring that emphasize a small school community, a positive school climate, cultural sensitivity, and building peer relationships with students and with teachers appear to encourage greater connectedness, thus reducing bullying behaviors. School cultures that nurture character and moral development are appealing in nature and are staffed with adults committed to exemplifying positive values.

HOW TO RECOGNIZE THE PROBLEM OF BULLYING AND DEVELOP AN ANTI-BULLYING POLICY

In preceding chapters we have laid out information about the bullying problem from elementary school through high school, looked at intervention and prevention resources for each of these levels, and considered how all adults can cooperate with parents and schools to reduce the bullying problem. Now, we must address the need to recognize the problem of bullying and to develop an anti-bullying policy.

Recognize the Problem of Bullying

One of the first steps that school faculty should take is gather information about bullying incidents and behaviors on its campus. This can be done easily by administering simple surveys, such as the ones that we have included in appendix B. The student survey will help the school identify how often children see bullying, how often they are bullied, the kinds of bullying that are occurring, and locations where bullying is happening. The teacher survey is also an important step in the data gathering process, because, as we have discussed earlier, teachers and children often have quite different perceptions of bullying at school. All of this is important information, because the results help a school structure an anti-bullying program around the specific needs of the school.

Develop an Anti-Bullying Policy

All schools have a school discipline policy, code of conduct, or a behavior management policy, but unfortunately most schools today do not have anti-bullying policies. Some policies mention bullying specifically, others include it with policies against hazing, harassment, or other forms of misconduct. In creating an anti-bullying policy for your school, begin by sharing summary findings from the survey with the school community. Then create a specific group of teachers, parents, and students to draft an anti-bullying policy.

The anti-bullying policy should provide general guidelines and should contain the following components (Rigby 2001, p. 24):

- A strong statement against bullying
- A definition of bullying
- A declaration of the rights of students and school personnel to be free from bullying and, when bullied, to be supported
- A statement of the responsibilities of individuals within the school community to not bully others, to discourage bullying when it occurs, and to provide support to those who are victimized
- A general description of consequences for bullying behavior (worded, for example, to say that the severity of bullying will be assessed and appropriate action taken, which may include the use of contacting parents, requiring counseling, and imposing sanctions such as detention, and in extreme cases suspension from school)
- An evaluation component

See sample anti-bullying policies in appendix C.

WHERE DO WE GO FROM HERE?

The answer is simple: we put our knowledge to use. To do this, we identify the extent of the problem on our campus, construct an all-school anti-bully policy, and begin the work of creating a school that is safe for all children and adults. We create a school where each individual is highly valued and respected and where student achievement is optimum.

As we have discussed throughout this book, bullying is a problem for all of our children—the bully, the bullied, and the bystander. Bullying does not just create unhappy moments for children at school; it can be the precursor to devastating acts of violence, such as what happened at Columbine High School. It can lead to life-long depression, dysfunctional relationships, imprisonment, and suicide. At the very least, bullying creates momentary sadness or discomfort; at the worst, it can lead to death.

Bullying behavior is unacceptable. We agree. Now it is time to do something about it.

REFERENCES

Agron, J. (1999). Safe havens. *American School and University* 71, 18–24.

Bowles, S. (2001). Educators try to establish anti-bullying policies. *USA Today*, April 17, 4A.

Harold, E. (2002). Harassment causes long-term pain. *USA Today*, October 4, 13A.

Harris, 3., and J. Harris (2001). Youth violence and suggestions for schools to reduce the violence. *Journal of At-Risk Issues* 7(2), 21–27.

Hewitt, P. (2002). Seeking tolerance. *Houston Chronicle*, April 4, A21.

Rigby, K. (1996). *Bullying in schools: And what to do about it.* London: Jessica Kingsley.

———— (2001). *Stop the bullying: A handbook for schools.* Camberwell: Australian Council for Educational Research.

APPENDIX A

STAR PLEDGE

Students: Tell an Adult Right Away!

I want _____ to be a place where all students feel safe and treat each other with respect. I will not bully, tease, or hurt anyone. If I hear bullying or teasing, I will tell the person to stop and report it to an adult. I will tell an adult right away if I hear anyone threaten another person. I will immediately tell an adult if a student brings something to school that could hurt someone.

_____   _____
Student Signature   Date

_____   _____
Parent Signature   Date

APPENDIX B

STUDENT AND
TEACHER SURVEYS TO IDENTIFY
BULLYING ON CAMPUS

STUDENT SURVEY (REV. 11/02)

Please do not put your name on this paper. Your answers should remain anonymous.

Section A

1. What is your gender?   a) male   b) female

2. Are you   a) Black   b) Hispanic   c) White   d) Other?

3. What is your grade level?   a) 6th   b) 7th   c) 8th   d) 9th

Bullying is when someone or a group of people repeatedly hurt or frighten someone weaker than themselves for no good reason. This may be done in different ways: by hurtful teasing, threatening actions or gestures, name calling, leaving people out of activities on purpose, spreading rumors about someone, stealing, hitting or kicking, or harassing sexually.

4. How often do you notice the following kinds of bullying at school?
   a) teasing in an unpleasant way   never   sometimes   often
   b) calling people hurtful names   never   sometimes   often

c) being left out on purpose	never	sometimes	often
d) threatening with harm	never	sometimes	often
e) hitting or kicking	never	sometimes	often
f) having things stolen	never	sometimes	often
g) spreading rumors	never	sometimes	often
h) harassing sexually	never	sometimes	often

5. Have you noticed bullying going on in this school in any of these places?

a) in the classroom	never	sometimes	often
b) at recess or break	never	sometimes	often
c) at lunch	never	sometimes	often
d) in the restroom	never	sometimes	often
e) in the hallways	never	sometimes	often
f) on the way to school	never	sometimes	often
g) on the way home from school	never	sometimes	often
h) at extracurricular events	never	sometimes	often
i) at initiations of clubs and teams	never	sometimes	often

6. When at school how safe do you feel from being bullied?
   a) rarely   b) sometimes   c) usually   d) always

Section B

Now, we would like to know how often *you* have been bullied by other students at school within the past year. Remember: it is *not* bullying when two students of about the same strength fight or quarrel. Bullying is when a stronger person or group of persons deliberately and repeatedly hurts someone who is weaker.

7. How often *within this past year* have you been bullied in any way by another student or group of students?
   a) at least once a week   b) at least once a month   c) never

8. How often were *you* bullied this year at school in the following ways?

a) teased in an unpleasant way	never	sometimes	often
b) called hurtful names	never	sometimes	often
c) left out of things on purpose	never	sometimes	often
d) threatened with harm	never	sometimes	often

e) hit or kicked	never	sometimes	often
f) had your things stolen	never	sometimes	often
g) rumors spread about you	never	sometimes	often
h) harassed sexually	never	sometimes	often

9. After being bullied, how have you generally felt about it?
a) I'm sad and miserable.
b) I'm angry.
c) It doesn't really bother me.
d) I have never been bullied.

10. Have you ever stayed away from school because of bullying?
a) Yes, I have stayed home from school more than twice because of bullying.
b) Yes, I have stayed home from school once or twice because of bullying.
c) No, but I've thought about staying home from school.
d) No, I've never thought of staying home from school.

11. Have you *told* any of the following persons about being bullied? (Circle as many as you have told.)
a) mother   b) father   c) sibling   d) friend
e) teacher   f) principal   g) counselor

12. What happened after you told someone about being bullied at school?
a) I was bullied, but I never told anyone.
b) I told, and it got worse.
c) I told, and the situation didn't change.
d) I told, and things got better.

Section C

13. Do you think that administrators at this school are interested in trying to stop bullying?
a) never   b) sometimes   c) usually   d) always

14. Do you think that teachers at this school are interested in trying to stop bullying?
a) never   b) sometimes   c) usually   d) always

15. Do you think that parents at this school are interested in trying to stop bullying?

   a) never   b) sometimes   c) usually   d) always

16. Do you think that students, teachers, administrators, and parents should work together to stop bullying?

   a) no   b) I'm not sure   c) yes

17. Would you be interested in talking about the problem of bullying at your school with other students to see what can be done about stopping it?

   a) no   b) maybe   c) yes

18. Please make one suggestion that would help your school decrease the problem of bullying:

_____

_____

SCHOOL PERSONNEL SURVEY: TEACHERS, COUNSELORS, ADMINISTRATORS (REV. 11/02)

Bullying is when a more powerful person or group repeatedly and deliberately hurt another person who is weaker. This does not include fighting or quarreling between people of roughly equal power or strength. The hurtful actions of bullying may be physical (hitting) or verbal (teasing, name calling, stealing). Bullying may also be indirect, as when a group of people sets out to exclude and isolate somebody, spread rumors about them, or threaten them. Bullying can also include sexual harassment.

Section A

1. What is your gender?   a) male   b) female

2. What is your age?   a) 21–30   b) 31–40   c) 41–50   d) 51+

3. What is your position at this school?
a) teacher   b) counselor   c) administrator   d) other

4. How often do you notice the following kinds of bullying at school among students?

a) teasing in an unpleasant way	never	sometimes	often
b) calling people hurtful names	never	sometimes	often
c) being left out of things on purpose	never	sometimes	often
d) threatening with harm	never	sometimes	often
e) hitting or kicking	never	sometimes	often
f) having things stolen	never	sometimes	often
g) spreading rumors	never	sometimes	often
h) harassing sexually	never	sometimes	often

5. Have you noticed bullying going on in this school in any of these places?

a) in the classroom	never	sometimes	often
b) at recess or break	never	sometimes	often
c) at lunch	never	sometimes	often
d) in the restroom	never	sometimes	often
e) in the hallways	never	sometimes	often

f) on the way to school	never	sometimes	often
g) on the way home from school	never	sometimes	often
h) at extracurricular events	never	sometimes	often
i) at initiations of clubs and teams	never	sometimes	often

6. How safe is your school for students who find it hard to defend themselves from bullying from other students?
a) rarely safe   b) sometimes safe   c) usually safe   d) always safe

7. Do you think that school personnel at your school are interested in trying to stop bullying?
a) never   b) sometimes   c) usually   d) always

8. Do you personally try to stop bullying when you see it happening?
a) never   b) sometimes   c) usually   d) always

9. To what extent have you personally discussed the issue of bullying at school with any class or student?
a) never   b) occasionally   c) fairly often   d) frequently

10. Have students informed you that they have been bullied while at school?
a) never   b) occasionally   c) fairly often   d) frequently

Section B

Here are some proposals that have been made to decrease bullying in schools. For each, indicate whether you a) strongly disagree, b) disagree, c) neither agree nor disagree, d) agree, or e) strongly agree.

11. A school policy should be developed focusing on what the school community will do to decrease bullying.
    a   b   c   d   e

12. Stopping bullying is a matter for *all* staff.
    a   b   c   d   e

13. Some training of staff is needed to deal with bullying.
    a   b   c   d   e

14. Designated individuals, for example, assistant principals, should be responsible for dealing with bullying.

    a   b   c   d   e

15. Some form of punishment should be applied *immediately and automatically* to students who bully others.

    a   b   c   d   e

16. Students bullying another person should *first* be counseled, not punished, and given the opportunity to put things right.

    a   b   c   d   e

17. More rigorous monitoring by staff of bullying is needed.

    a   b   c   d   e

18. Teachers should discuss bullying with their class.

    a   b   c   d   e

19. Teach curriculum to frequently victimized students to develop their social skills and to become more assertive.

    a   b   c   d   e

20. What suggestions would you make to reduce bullying at your school?

    _____

    _____

Note: These surveys are copyrighted to Sandra Harris and Garth Petrie (11/2002) and adapted from K. Rigby (1997): *Peer relations assessment questionnaire: The professional reading guide for educational administrators*, ed. Barrington Thomas (Adelaide: University of South Australia).

APPENDIX C

SAMPLE SCHOOL
ANTI-BULLYING POLICIES

8260 BULLYING (CF 8018) 8260:
BULLYING PROHIBITED IN MICHIGAN

Bullying is a form of harassment. For the purposes of this policy, "bullying" is defined as: "The repeated intimidation of others by the real or threatened infliction of physical, verbal, written, electronically transmitted, or emotional abuse, or through attacks on the property of another. It may include, but not be limited to, actions such as verbal taunts, name-calling and put-downs, including ethnically based or gender based verbal put-downs, extortion of money or possessions, and exclusion from peer groups within school." Such conduct is disruptive of the educational process and, therefore, bullying is not acceptable behavior in this District, and is prohibited.

Students who engage in any act of bullying while at school, at any school function, in connection to or with any District sponsored activity or event, or while enroute to or from school are subject to disciplinary action, up to and including suspension or expulsion. As may be required by law, law enforcement officials shall be notified of bullying incidents.

The Superintendent shall develop administrative regulations and programs that will increase awareness of the problem of bullying, and train teachers and other staff to effectively intervene if bullying is witnessed in their presence or brought to their attention. In designing administrative regulations and anti-bullying programs or strategies, the Superintendent should consult with the greater school community, including students.

This policy shall not be interpreted to prohibit a reasoned and civil exchange of opinions, or debate, that is protected by state or federal law.

Approved: LEGAL REF. "Policies on Bullying," Michigan State Board of Education, 7-19-01; *Tinker v Des Moines Independent School District*, 393 US 503(1969). See also: *Saxe v College Area School District*, 240 F3d 200(CA 3, 2001). Mr. Robert Ebersole, J.D., Assistant Director of Bylaw and Policy Services, author. Contact the Massachusetts Association of School Boards Bylaw and Policy Services office at (517) 327-5928 or email an inquiry to bscharffe@masb.org or bebersole@masb.org. Source: Michigan Department of Education. Michigan Safe Schools. Available online: http://www.michigansafeschools.org/models/bullying.htm. Accessed: October 13, 2002.

SAMPLE BULLYING POLICY IN DENVER PUBLIC SCHOOLS

Proposed Policy: Bullying Prevention and Education (Policy JICDE)

The mission of the Denver Public Schools, the center of learning for the community, is to guarantee that our children and youth acquire knowledge, skills and values to become self-sufficient citizens and life-long learners. We can achieve this mission by providing personalized learning experience in an environment that is safe, conducive to learning and free from unnecessary disruption.

The Denver Public Schools supports a secure school environment, conducive to teaching and learning in an environment free from threat, harassment and any type of bullying behavior. The Board of Education is adopting this policy to promote consistency of approach and to help create an environment in which all types of bullying are regarded as unacceptable.

Definition: Bullying is defined "as any written or verbal expression, or physical act or gesture or pattern thereof, that is intended to cause distress upon one or more students in the school, on school grounds, in school vehicles, at a designated school bus stop, or at school activities or sanctioned events" CRS 22-32-109.1 (2)(a)(X).

Consequences: Students who engage in any act of bullying are subject to appropriate disciplinary action in accordance with District Policy JK (VI) pertaining to discipline procedures and may include suspension, expulsion, or referral to law enforcement authorities. The severity and pattern, if any, of the bullying shall be taken into consideration when disciplinary decisions are made.

The Superintendent shall develop a comprehensive program to address bullying at all grade levels. The program shall be directed to accomplish the following goals:

- To send a clear message to students, staff, parents and community members that bullying will not be tolerated.
- To implement procedures for immediate intervention, investigation, and confrontation of students engaged in bullying behavior.
- To initiate programs to change the behavior of students engaged in bullying behaviors through reeducation on acceptable behavior, discussions, counseling and appropriate negative consequences.
- To develop and foster a productive partnership with parents and community members in order to help maintain a bully-free environment.
- To support victims of bullying by means of individual and peer counseling.
- To recognize and praise positive, supportive behaviors of students toward one another on a regular basis.

Adopted: LEGAL REFS.: C.r.s. 22-32-109.1(2)(a)(X); CROSS REFS.: JK, Student Conduct and Discipline.

Source: *Denver Public Schools* at http://www.dpsk12.org/proposed_policies/pp_jicde.shtml. Accessed October 14, 2002.

ADDITIONAL RESOURCES

APA Monitor On-line (1999). Bullying widespread in middle school, say three studies, at www.apa.org/monitor/oct99/cf3.html.

Ballard, M., T. Argus, and T. Remley (1999). Bullying and school violence: A proposed intervention. *NASSP Bulletin* 83(6–7), 38–47.

Banks, R. (1997). *Bullying in schools* (Report No. EDO-PS-97-17). Champaign, Ill.: Clearinghouse on Elementary and Early Childhood Education, at ericeece.org/pubs/digest/1997/banks97.html.

Boatwright, B., T. Mathis, and S. Smith-Rex (2000). *Getting equipped to stop bullying: A kid's survival kit for understanding and coping with violence in the schools.* Minneapolis, Minn.: Educational Media Corporation

Boivin, M., S. Hymel, and E. Hodges (2001). Toward a process view of peer rejection and harassment. In J. Juvonen and S. Graham (eds.), *Peer harassment in school: The plight of the vulnerable and victimized.* New York: Guilford Press.

Bowman, D. (2001). *At school, a cruel culture,* at www.edweek.org/ew/ew_printstory.cfm?slug+27taunts.h20.

Byrne, B. J. (1994). Bullies and victims in school settings with reference to some Dublin schools. *Irish Journal of Psychology* 15, 574–86.

Craig, W., and D. Peplar (1996). Understanding bullying at school: What can we do about it? In S. Miller, J. Brodine, and T. Miller (eds.), *Safe by design.* Seattle, Wash.: Committee for Children.

Crick, N., and J. Grotpeter (1995). Relational aggression, gender, and social-psychological adjustment. *Child Development* 66, 710–22.

Crick, N., and N. Werner (1998). Response decision processes in relational and overt aggression. *Child Development* 69, 1630–39.

Darling-Hammond, L. (1997). *The right to learn: A blueprint for creating schools that work.* San Francisco: Jossey-Bass.

Dietz, B. (1994). *Effects on subsequent heterosexual shyness and depression of peer victimization at school.* Paper presented at the International Conference on Children's Peer Relations. Institute of Social Research: University of South Australia, Adelaide.

Flannery, D., and M. Singer (1999). Exposure to violence and victimization at school. *Choices Briefs (4)*, Institute for Urban and Minority Education, Teachers College, Columbia University, at iume.tc.columbia.edu/choices/briefs/choices04.html.

Gilmartin, B. G. (1987). Peer group antecedents of severe love shyness in males. *Journal of Personality* 55, 467–89.

Harachi, T., R. Catalano, and J. Hawkins (1999). United States. In P. K. Smith et al. (eds.), *The nature of school bullying: A cross-national perspective.* London: Routledge.

Hellmich, N. (2002). Caught in the catty corner. *USA Today*, April 9, D1.

Hinde, R. (1986). Some implications of evolutionary theory and comparative data for the study of human prosocial and aggressive behaviour. In D. Olweus, J. Block, M., and Radke-Yarrow (eds.), *Development of antisocial and prosocial behavior: Research, theories, and issues.* Orlando, Fla.: Academic Press.

Juvonen, J., A. Nishina, and S. Graham (2001). Self-views versus peer perceptions of victim status among early adolescents. In J. Juvonen and S. Graham (eds.), *Peer harassment in school: The plight of the vulnerable and victimized.* New York: Guilford Press

Kazdin, A. (1993). Treatment of conduct disorder: Progress and direction in psychotherapy research. *Development and Psychopathology* 5, 277–310.

Kenney, D., and S. Watson (1999). *Crime in the schools: Reducing conflict with student problem solving.* National Institute of Justice Research in Brief. U.S. Department of Justice.

Kumpalainen, K., E. Rasanen, and I. Henttonen (1999). Children involved in bullying: Psychological disturbance and the persistence of the involvement. *Child Abuse & Neglect: The International Journal* 23(12), 1253–62.

Limber, S., et al. (1998). In M. Watts (ed.), *Cross-cultural perspectives on youth and violence: Contemporary studies in sociology,* vol. 18. Stamford, Conn.: Jai Press.

Lindsey, D. (2001). Is there anything left to say? *Salon.com News,* at www.salon.com/news/feature/2001/03/06/school_shootings/index.html.

Maeroff, G. (2000). A symbiosis of sorts: School violence and the media. *Choices Briefs* (7). Institute for Urban and Minority Education, Teachers College, Columbia University, at iume.tc.columbia.edu/choices/briefs/choice07.html.

McClellan, D. (1994). Research on multiage grouping: Implications for education. In P. Chase and J. Doan (eds.), *Full circle: A new look at multiage education*. Portsmouth, N.H.: Heinemann.

McClellan, D. (1997). Addressing the risk of bullying in mixed-age groups. *The Magnet Newsletter* 5(2), at www/uncg.edu/edu/ericcass/bullying/DOCS/magspr97.htm.

National Institute of Education (1978). *Violent schools-safe schools: The safe school study report to the Congress*. Washington, D.C.: U.S. Department of Education.

Oliver, R., J. Hoover, and R. Hazler (1994). The perceived roles of bullying in small-town Midwestern schools. *Journal of Counseling and Development* 72(4), 410–19.

Olweus, D. (1997). Bully/victim problems in school: Facts and intervention. *European Journal of Psychology of Education* 12(4), 495–510.

Osofsky, J. D. (ed.). (1997). *Children in a violent society*. New York: Guilford.

Pelligrini, A. D. (1989). Elementary school children's rough-and-tumble play. *Early Childhood Research Quarterly* 4(2), 245–61.

Pelligrini, A. D., and M. Bartini (2000). A longitudinal study of bullying, victimization, and peer affiliation during the transition from primary school to middle school. *American Educational Research Journal* 37(3), 699–725.

Petersen, G. J. (1997) Looking at the big picture: School administrators and violence reduction. *Journal of School Leadership* 7(5), 456–79.

Peterson, M. (1993). Tiny tyrants. *Minnesota Parent*, October, 17–19.

Sauerwein, K. (1995). Violence and young children. *Executive Educator* 17(3), 23–26.

Smith, P. (1999). England and Wales. In P. Smith et al. (eds.), *The nature of school bullying: A cross-national perspective*. London: Routledge.

Smith, P., and P. Brain (2000). Bullying in schools: Lessons from two decades of research. *Aggressive Behavior* 26, 1–9.

Smith, P., et al. (eds.) (1999). *The nature of school bullying: A cross-national perspective*. London: Routledge.

Smith, P., and S. Sharp (1994). *School bullying: Insights and perspectives*. London: Routledge.

Vail, K. (1999). Words that wound. *American School Board Journal* 186(9), 26–28.

Viadero, D. (1997). Bullies beware. *Education Week* 16(35), 19–21.

Vossekuil, B., et al. (2000). *United States Secret Service safe school initiative: An interim report on the prevention of targeted violence in schools*. Washington, D.C.: U.S. Secret Service, National Threat Assessment Center.

Whitney, I., P. Smith, and D. Thompson (1994). Bullying and children with special education needs. In P. Smith and S. Sharp (eds.), *School bullying: Insights and perspectives*. London: Routledge.

INDEX

ABOUT THE AUTHORS

Sandra Harris (Ph.D., University of Texas at Austin) has more than thirty years of experience as a teacher and administrator in private and public schools, and is currently assistant professor of educational leadership at Stephen F. Austin State University in Nacogdoches, Texas, where she teaches in the principal preparation and doctoral programs. Dr. Harris has published numerous articles in journals and book chapters and is a reviewer for several educational journals. She has co-authored two books for ScarecrowEducation, *A School for Every Child: School Choice in America Today* and *Standards-Based Leadership: A Case Study Book for Superintendents*. In addition, Dr. Harris has presented on the topic of bullying at many state and national conferences, including the University Council of Educational Administration, National Council of Professors of Educational Administration, and American Educational Research Association.

Dr. Harris became interested in school violence and bullying because of her belief that every child should have a safe, positive experience at school. Her other research interests are school reform, the principalship, and standards-based leadership.

Garth F. Petrie (Ed.D., Indiana University, Bloomington) has fourteen years of public school experience and has spent thirty years as a university professor. He is currently professor at Stephen F. Austin State University in Nacogdoches, Texas, where he teaches in the doctoral program. He has also published numerous articles in journals and book chapters, and is a reviewer for three educational journals.

Dr. Petrie became interested in bullying because one of his grand-daughters has been bullied over a three-year period at school and it has seriously affected her grades and happiness. His other research interests are discipline, children's violence, a principal's use of power, and change influences in public schools. He is presently working with several area public schools on improving instruction.